500 WEDDING RINGS

500 WEDDING RINGS

CELEBRATING A CLASSIC SYMBOL OF COMMITMENT

A Division of
Sterling Publishing Co., Inc.
New York / London

EDITOR: **Marthe Le Van**

ART DIRECTOR: **Jackie Kerr**

COVER DESIGNER: **Cindy LaBreacht**

ASSISTANT EDITORS: **Cassie Moore,
Mark Bloom**

ASSOCIATE ART DIRECTOR: **Shannon Yokeley**

ART PRODUCTION ASSISTANT: **Jeff Hamilton**

EDITORIAL ASSISTANCE: **Dawn Dillingham,
Rosemary Kast**

PROOFREADER: **Jessica Boing**

FRONT COVER
Daphne Milne Groos
Untitled, 2004

SPINE
Geoffrey Giles
Ours, 2005

BACK COVER, TOP LEFT
Sasha Samuels
Temple Ring, 2002

BACK COVER, TOP RIGHT
Ryota Sakamoto
Aros, 2005

BACK COVER, BOTTOM LEFT
Adam Neeley
The Sculpture Ring, 2006

BACK COVER, BOTTOM right
Hagen Gamisch
Animalia, 2006

FRONT FLAP, TOP
Michele Mercaldo
Sapphire Diamond Ring, 2005

FRONT FLAP, BOTTOM
Robin Cust
Untitled, 2006

BACK FLAP
Adam Neeley
Trio, 2006

TITLE PAGE
Adam Neeley
Fiore, 2006

OPPOSITE
Cassandra L. Foral
Mine Is Bigger Than Yours, 2006

Library of Congress Cataloging-in-Publication Data

500 wedding rings : celebrating a classic symbol of commitment. -- 1st ed.
    p. cm.
  Includes index.
  ISBN-13: 978-1-60059-054-2 (pb-with flaps : alk. paper)
  ISBN-10: 1-60059-054-3 (pb-with flaps : alk. paper)
  1. Jewelry--Design. 2. Rings--Pictorial works. 3. Betrothal. 4.
Marriage customs and rites. I. Title: Five hundred wedding rings.
  NK7305.A17 2007
  739.27'82--dc22

                              200702489

10 9 8 7 6 5 4 3 2 1

First Edition

Published by Lark Books, A Division of
Sterling Publishing Co., Inc.
387 Park Avenue South, New York, N.Y. 10016

Text © 2007, Lark Books
Photography © 2007 Artist/Photographer as noted

Distributed in Canada by Sterling Publishing,
c/o Canadian Manda Group, 165 Dufferin Street
Toronto, Ontario, Canada M6K 3H6

Distributed in the United Kingdom by GMC Distribution Services,
Castle Place, 166 High Street, Lewes, East Sussex, England BN7 1XU

Distributed in Australia by Capricorn Link (Australia) Pty Ltd.,
P.O. Box 704, Windsor, NSW 2756 Australia

If you have questions or comments about this book, please contact:
Lark Books
67 Broadway
Asheville, NC 28801
(828) 253-0467

Manufactured in China

ISBN 13: 978-1-60059-054-2
ISBN 10: 1-60059-054-3

For information about custom editions, special sales, premium and corporate
purchases, please contact Sterling Special Sales Department at 800-805-5489
or specialsales@sterlingpub.com.

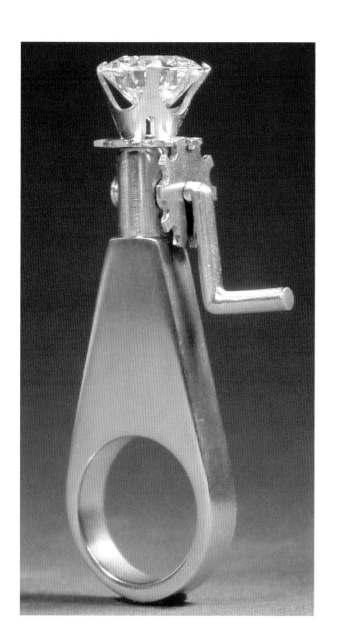

Contents

Esther Davies
Untitled | 2002

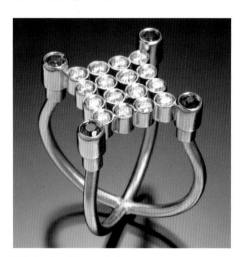

Michele Mercaldo
Sapphire Diamond Ring | 2005

Introduction

My wedding ring was created five years after I was married. My husband and I had happily worn simple silver bands until one day, without warning, something changed. The time became right for us to make a visual statement to the world about our union. Perhaps, like a good pot of gumbo, our relationship had to simmer and our flavors merge over time in order to develop the character we felt ready to share publicly through a more personalized symbol.

Choosing the right jeweler was easy. We picked a dear friend whose style we adored. The diamonds were to be recycled from my grandmother's dinner ring, a very beautiful but very dated traditional setting. The first step was removing the stones. That there were 22 diamonds to work with was a thrilling discovery; that they were all of varying sizes was a challenging one. We worked together on the design, selecting the right strength and colors of metal, the right thickness of the band, the right placement for the stones. My husband and I wore mock-ups for several months to make sure the band's square shape would be comfortable. The collaborative process was definitely thrilling, but it did not compare to the ecstasy I felt when I first glimpsed the finished rings.

Fancying myself a nonconformist, I didn't want to believe in the power of wedding rings. I thought they were bourgeois status symbols like overpriced cars and giant homes. The media bombardment of ads featuring sugary slogans and unblemished models in romantic locales didn't help me swallow the hype. But one spring evening our jeweler friend rang the doorbell. She had come to deliver our custom handmade rings. Although I had been deeply moved by artwork in the past, I never knew an object could have such a profound personal effect. My conversion to the power of this age-old form was instantaneous and complete.

You may be surprised to learn that today's most popular wedding ring set—a diamond solitaire and matching bands—is a relatively modern development. Ancient civilizations living along the fertile plains of the Nile River were the first people to form tokens of commitment. They twisted and braided grasses and reeds from the riverbanks into symbolic finger rings. Iron was preferred by the early Romans, who believed this strong material reflected the strength of their unions. Iron continues being used to this day, as seen in the work of Cappy Counard (page 30), Robin Cust (right, bottom), and Rob Jackson (page 123).

Different types of metal and designs fell in and out of fashion from the Middle Ages right up until the mid-twentieth century. The puzzle ring, now an everyday accessory, was devised in Turkey as a wedding band with a purpose. Should the wearer desire to be unfaithful, she would have to remove the ring and then be clever enough to reassemble its parts after her indiscretion. Yael Friedman's *Marriage as a Puzzle* (right, top) is an extraordinary contemporary version. Community rings, used during Jewish wedding ceremonies but not worn every day, suggest the architectural shape of a temple. Most have slanted roofs or Moorish domes with a chimney or slot into which a written prayer for the couple is placed. Esther Davies's ring (left, top), Vicki Ambery-Smith's *Olomuc Synagogue* (page 361), and Dorit Bouskila Dehan's *Kol Sason Vekol Simcha* (page 247) continue this tradition.

The wedding ring has evolved in form countless times. Its purpose, however, has remained unchanged: to signify unending union. The wedding rings selected for this collection were designed and created by contemporary jewelers from all over the globe. Each piece is as unique as its maker, and the diversity will astound and inspire you. In Adam Neeley's *Trio* (page 341), Michele Mercaldo's *Sapphire Diamond Ring* (left, bottom), and Philippe Tournaire's *Opera Ring* (page 22), traditional diamonds and precious metals are given a more avant-garde appeal. Astonishing technical virtuosity can be seen in the mokume gane wedding rings of George Sawyer (page 17) and James E. Binnion (page 16) and in the married metals of Geoffrey D. Giles (page 14). Some rings, like Georgia Vandewater's *Joined* (page 44), are conceived to fit together, marrying each other to form a whole. Others, like Annie Tung's *Divorce Ring: A Broken Nest, a Broken Ring* (page 196), are intentionally deconstructed. Several of the wedding rings are meant to last only for a single hour or a single day. Such fleeting expressions can be seen in the newspaper constructions of Elisa Gulminelli's *One-Day Commitment Wedding Ring* (page 332), the ice carving of Glynis Gardner's *Love You Long Time* (page 131), and Reneé Zettle-Sterling's *Cherished Rings, Cherished Earth* (page 130), formed from compressed earth. Perhaps these temporal pieces lead us back, full circle, to the ancient Egyptians braiding reeds on the banks of the Nile.

Each morning, putting on my wedding ring serves as a gentle reminder of the choice I have made to experience my life in unison with another person. It is intensely rewarding that a jeweler was able to capture the spirit of my relationship in a tangible work of art. *500 Wedding Rings* presents this type of meaningful work created by an incredible range of talented individuals. The value of their one-of-a-kind rings exceeds dollars and cents. These rings are more than status symbols. They are soul symbols, meant for lovers everywhere.

Marthe Le Van

Yael Friedman
Marriage as a Puzzle | 2006

Robin Cust
Untitled | 2006

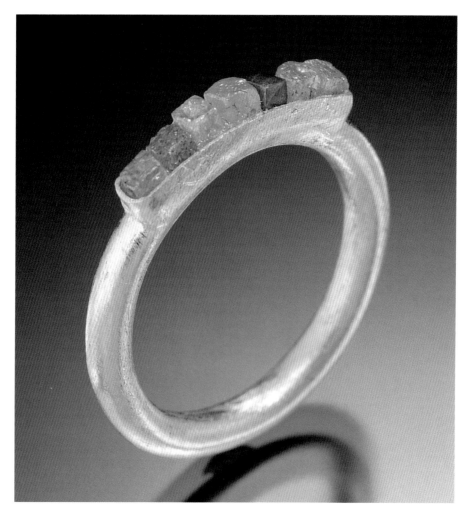

April Higashi

Raw Diamond Channel Ring | 2004

2.5 X 1.9 X 0.3 CM
Raw diamonds, 18-karat gold

PHOTO BY HAP SAKWA

ON EACH *anniversary, celebrate with a new diamond. Each ring can receive an additional diamond of the same size every year.* —SY

Sayumi Yokouchi
Untitled | 2003

LEFT, 1.6 X 1.6 X 0.3 CM;
RIGHT, 1.8 X 1.8 X 0.4 CM

Diamonds, 18-karat yellow gold;
set, forged, hammered

PHOTO BY RALPH GABRINER

MY WORK *expresses the quiet elegance found in things often overlooked, the idea that transcendence can be found in what's common and small.* —DD

Deborrah Daher
Wrap Ring, Pieces Ring, Wrap Ring | 1998

CENTER, 1.2 X 1.2 CM
14-karat yellow gold, sterling
silver; fabricated, forged

PHOTO BY RALPH GABRINER

Michele Mercaldo

Cognac Diamond Ring | 2006

2.5 X 1.9 X 1.9 CM

18-karat yellow gold, cognac diamond, diamonds

PHOTO BY ROBERT DIAMANTE

COURTESY OF MICHELE MERCALDO CONTEMPORARY JEWELRY DESIGN,
BOSTON, MASSACHUSETTS

THE EVERCHANGING

Ring is about metal and the interaction between wearer and artist. It is about pure gold and how it is 100-percent recyclable without losing its properties. The ring is worn for a time, and then returned to me once the owners' lives either change significantly or need visual encouragement to do so. The golden ingot transforms through melting and forging to become a new ring. Purity and weight are maintained, as is the aesthetic of unearthed treasure. An album accompanies the ring that records five generations of changes with photo documentation and specifications. —JB

Jana Brevick
The Everchanging Ring | 1999–present
2.8 X 0.5 CM
24-karat fine gold
PHOTO BY DOUGLAS YAPLE

So Young Park
Untitled | 2005

2 X 2 X 1.5 CM
22-karat yellow gold, 18-karat white gold, diamonds;
hammered, soldered, hand fabricated, set

Geoffrey D. Giles

Ours | 2005

LARGER, 2.3 X 2.3 X 0.6 CM; SMALLER, 2 X 2 X 0.5 CM

18-karat yellow gold, 18-karat palladium white gold,
diamonds; married metal, fabricated, brushed surface
embellishments, set

PHOTO BY TAYLOR DABNEY

THESE RINGS *are simply distinct with the contrast of oxidized sterling silver and 18-karat yellow gold. The added subtle texture offers another hint of elegance.* —TKFB

Tavia K. F. Brown

Sans Fringe Wedding Set | 2005

LEFT, 2.5 X 2.5 X 0.6 CM

Sterling silver, 18-karat yellow gold; lost wax cast, fabricated, textured

PHOTO BY TAYLOR DABNEY

James E. Binnion

Mokume Wedding Ring | 2004

0.9 X 0.2 CM

14-karat palladium white gold, sterling silver, 18-karat yellow gold; mokume gane

Photo by Hap Sakwa

George Sawyer

Primitive Symmetry | 2000

2.5 X 0.6 X 2.5 CM

14-karat gray gold, sterling silver,
22-karat yellow gold; pattern matched
edge grain mokume gane, fabricated

PHOTO BY PETER LEE

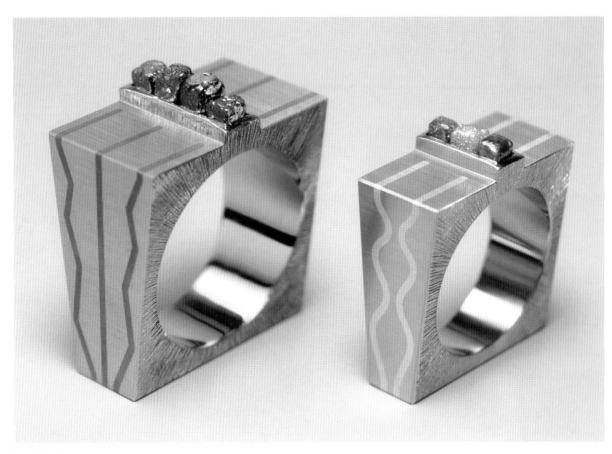

Pat Pruitt

Untitled | 2007

LEFT, 2.9 X 2.4 X 1.5 CM; RIGHT, 2.4 X 2.1 X 1 CM

Stainless steel, industrial diamonds, fine silver; machined, hammer set, senzogan, chisel texture, oxidized, sanded

PHOTO BY ARTIST

Ryota Sakamoto

Aros | 2005

2.2 X 2.2 X 0.6 CM

Titanium, duralumin; expansive
diffusion bonded, machined

PHOTO BY ARTIST

Meghan Gillan

Give and Take | 2006

LEFT, 2.2 X 0.5 CM; RIGHT, 2.4 X 0.6 CM

Silver, stainless steel; cut, rolled,
hydraulically pressed, lathe turned

PHOTO BY ARTIST

THE COUPLE *who commissioned these rings
courted for eight years prior to marriage.
It was important for them to have a design that
signified their deep connection. The rings are
meant to celebrate the effort of giving and taking
in a relationship; the strength of the stainless
steel and the tight fit represent the strength it
takes to keep it all together.* —MG

THE SCULPTURE RING *resonates with its wearer's individuality. Why can't a wedding ring be a work of art?* —AN

Adam Neeley
The Sculpture Ring | 2006

3 X 4.5 X 2 CM
14-karat white gold, diamond; cast

PHOTO BY HAP SAKWA

Philippe Tournaire

Opera Ring | 2000

2.4 X 0.7 X 0.2 CM

Platinum, diamonds, 18-karat white gold

PHOTO BY ARTIST

Hisako Tsukamoto

Penetration | 2006

2.4 X 4.4 X 0.9 CM
Titanium, diamonds; machined

PHOTOS BY ARTIST

Meister & Co.

Meister Wedding Bands, Phantastics | 2006

0.7 X 0.3 CM
Platinum, diamonds

PHOTO BY ARTIST

Hisako Tsukamoto

Hub Ring | 2004

2.3 X 2.3 X 0.8 CM
Titanium; machined

PHOTO BY ARTIST

Sawako Hirayama

Stream | 2005

2.2 X 2.2 X 0.7 CM

Platinum, white gold; mokume gane

PHOTO BY ARTIST

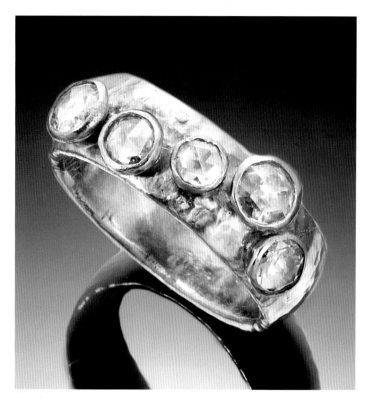

Gurhan

Journey Diamond Ring | 2006

2.5 X 2.2 X 0.6 CM
Platinum, white rose-cut diamonds;
hand fabricated, hammered

PHOTO BY RALPH GABRINER

Barbara Paganin

Epicarpo | 1998

LEFT, 2.7 X 1.4 CM

Fine gold, 18-karat gold, oxidized
sterling silver, freshwater pearls

PHOTO BY ARTIST

Beate Klockmann

King of the Day, Queen of the Night | 2005

EACH, 2.5 X 1.5 CM
18-karat gold, tantalum, white gold

PHOTO BY ARTIST

Cappy Counard
Untitled | 2006

LEFT, 2.3 X 2.3 X 0.7 CM; RIGHT, 2.2 X 2 X 0.7 CM
Sapphire, wrought iron, 18-karat gold; fabricated

PHOTO BY ARTIST

Ruudt Peters

Weddingring | 1987

LARGEST, 2.2 X 2.2 X 0.6 CM

18-karat gold, tantalum

PHOTO BY ROB VERSLUYS

THE RINGS *are a play on the traditional ideas and notions attached to engagement rings—size, value, and achievement.* —SM

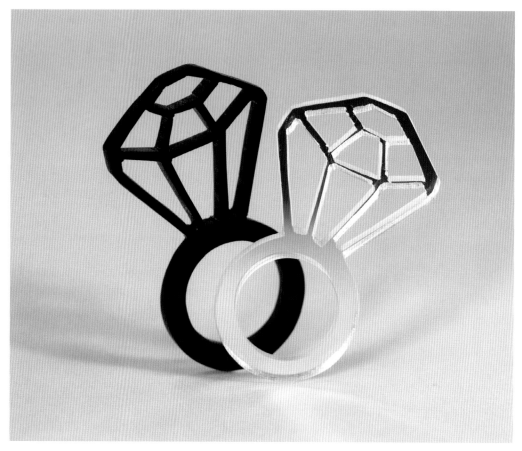

Sylvie Markovina
Diamond Rings | 2006

EACH, 5 X 2.7 X 0.3 CM
Acrylic; saw pierced

PHOTO BY JAMES GOODE

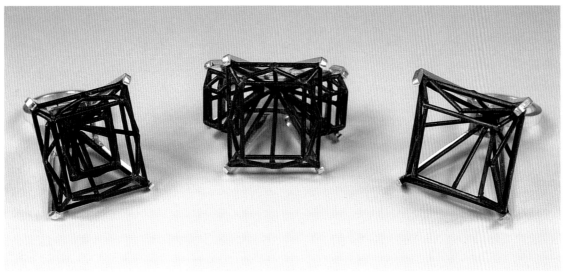

Laura Coddens

Engagement Series | 2006

LEFT AND CENTER, 5 X 2.5 X 2.5 CM;
RIGHT, 5 X 3.8 X 2.5 CM

Sterling silver, steel; fabricated

PHOTOS BY CAROLINE GORE

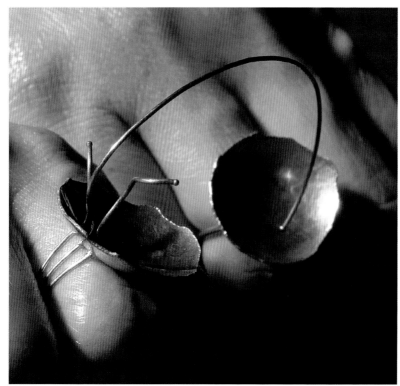

Hsueh-Ying Wu
Touching | 2007

3 X 2.6 X 2.5 CM
Gold; forged, hand fabricated

PHOTOS BY CHIN-TING CHIU

Vinograd Yasmin

Untitled | 2005

2.7 X 2.7 X 3.2 CM

Plutonic stone, 18-karat gold; lost wax cast

PHOTO BY SOCHOVOLSKI MEIDAD

Fabrizio Tridenti

Year on the Square | 2006

2.4 X 2 X 0.8 CM

Bronze, aluminum; fused

PHOTO BY LUCIANO DI LELLO

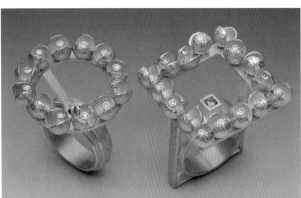

Liaung Chung Yen

Flourishing #6 & #7 | 2006

AVERAGE, 3.5 X 2.5 X 2.5 CM

18-karat gold, diamonds,
brown diamonds; fabricated

PHOTOS BY ARTIST

Patrick Malotki

Heart Wedding Rings | 2002

2.1 X 0.5 CM
18-karat gold

PHOTO BY MARKUS GELDHAUSER

Karl Fritsch

Untitled | 2005

2.5 X 2.5 X 0.5 CM
Gold; cast

PHOTO BY ARTIST

THE PECULIARITY
*of my work is the
combination and mixing of
old traditional handicraft
and newest technological
processes. In my opinion,
it's also important in your
personal life and marriage
to live the good things of
old traditions, but also to
embrace the new movements
and emotions.* —HG

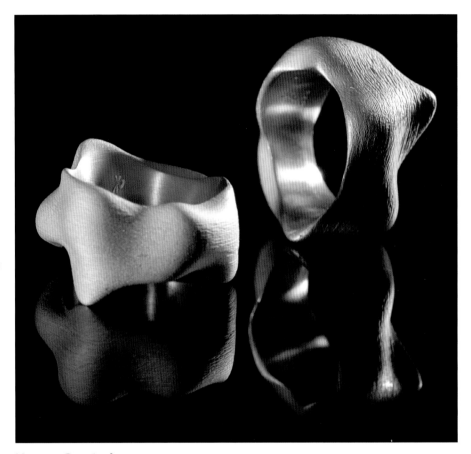

Hagen Gamisch
Animalia | 2006

2.7 X 2.7 X 1.5 CM
Silver, fine gold; CAD, sand cast

PHOTO BY ISOLDE GOLDERER

39

Todd Reed

Untitled | 2006

2 X 0.3 CM

18-karat yellow gold, raw diamond cubes,
brilliant cut diamonds; forged, fabricated

PHOTO BY AZADPHOTO.COM

IN ALCHEMY, "circle within a circle" is the symbol for the sun. High-karat gold is also symbolic of the sun in many cultures. Combining symbolic materials with mutually supportive imagery is a fundamental aspect of goldsmithing an emotionally charged bridal ornament. —NA

Nanz Aalund

Solstice Wedding Ring | 2005

2.5 X 1.7 X 2 CM
Sterling silver, 22-karat yellow gold, diamond; roll printed with laser cut stencil, fabricated, bezel set

PHOTO BY JIM FORBES

Andy Cooperman

Skin Rings | 2004

LARGEST, 2.2 X 0.5 X 0.8 CM

14-karat white gold, 18-karat yellow gold,
14-karat rose gold; forged, fabricated

PHOTO BY DOUG YAPLE

Heather Kita

Rain | 2006

2.6 X 2.5 X 16 CM

18-karat yellow gold, brown diamond; cast

PHOTO BY BLASER PHOTOGRAPHY
COURTESY OF GOLDSMITH SILVERSMITH, INC., OMAHA, NEBRASKA

TWO WEDDING *rings, in the center of which sits a key holding the individuals together as one. When apart, there is a memory of what they are when together, and the key a memento.* —GV

Georgia Vandewater
Joined | 2005

2.3 X 2 X 0.1 CM
Stainless steel, 18-karat yellow gold;
cast, turned, milled, fabricated

PHOTOS BY ARTIST

Katsue Imoue

Tri-Color | 2006

2.2 X 2.2 X 1 CM

Platinum, white gold, tantalum, orange gold;
mokume gane, machined

PHOTO BY ARTIST

Satoshi Sorayama

Ladder | 2003

2.4 X 5.2 X 0.7 CM
Titanium, diamonds; machined,
assembled, oxidized

PHOTO BY ARTIST

THIS RING *represents matrimony, the basis of what a marriage is all about. The grooves represent the future; each of them stands for one year. Each groove is to be filled with a material that reflects or symbolizes the past year. In this manner the ring will steadily be filled with references to personal memories, experiences, and emotions. Over the years, a marriage will grow more complete, as does the ring.* —SC

Sabrina Cools
Our Life | 2006

LEFT, 0.6 X 0.2 X 2.3 CM;
RIGHT, 0.6 X 0.2 X 2.2 CM
Silver, gold; cast, drilled

PHOTO BY PHILIP SAJET

Benjamin Lignel
Act I: Set of Two Snappable Wedding Rings | 2002

2.4 X 4.9 X 0.3 CM
24-karat gold; lost wax cast, fabricated

PHOTO BY JOËL DEGEN

Jens Clausen

Protection | 2006

SQUARE, 2.3 X 2.3 X 1.2 CM;
CIRCULAR, 2.3 X 2 X 0.7 CM

Sterling silver, stainless
steel; mounted, turned,
milled, hand finished

PHOTOS BY ARTIST

Joanna Gollberg

No Less—You Are | 2003

EACH, 1 X 1 X 0.3 CM

18-karat yellow gold, 14-karat
white gold, diamonds

PHOTO BY ARTIST
PRIVATE COLLECTION

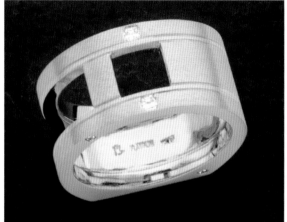

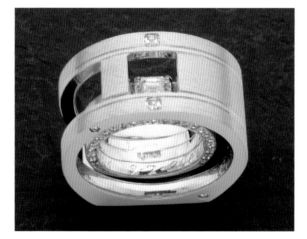

Marc Stiglitz

Interlocked Hearts Wedding Band Set | 2006

LARGER, 2.4 X 1.2 X 2.3 CM; SMALLER, 1.9 X 0.6 X 1.8 CM

Platinum, 14-karat yellow gold, Asscher-cut diamonds; hand forged, burnished, prong set, pavé set, hand engraved

PHOTOS BY GEORGE POST

Amy Renshaw

One Check Ring | 2006

0.4 X 0.2 CM

18-karat palladium white gold,
baguette diamond; set, polished

PHOTO BY TERENCE BOGUE

Ezra Satok-Wolman

Rough Diamond Engagement Ring | 2005

2.5 X 2.2 X 0.9 CM

18-karat red gold, rough diamond,
natural pink and blue diamonds;
tension set, riveted

PHOTO BY ARTIST

Christine Dhein

My Brother's Wedding Set | 2006

LARGEST, 2.5 X 2.5 X 0.8 CM

18-karat palladium white gold, diamonds;
wax carved, cast, channel set

PHOTO BY ARTIST

Philip Sajet

Infinity | 1980

2 X 4 X 0.3 CM

Pure gold, 18-karat gold

PHOTOS BY ARTIST
COLLECTION OF
MR. AND MRS. ROOZENDAAL-HENSELMANS

Daphne Milne Groos

Untitled | 2005

0.7 X 0.7 CM

18-karat yellow gold, diamond; sculpted, set

PHOTOS BY JAMES DEE

THIS RING *reminds me of the brushstroke mark made for the character for Zen. It is also based on a mobius strip which is never ending—a beautiful symbol of partnership.* —JB

Jane Bowden
Zen Ring | 2004

2.7 X 2.5 X 0.7 CM
22-karat gold; hand forged

PHOTO BY GRANT HANCOCK

Stuart Golder

Parallel Patchwork &
Patchwork Flash Rings | 2006

EACH, 0.9 X 2 X 2 CM

18-karat rose, yellow, white,
and green gold; constructed

PHOTO BY RALPH GABRINER

Louise Norrell

2 Part Wedding Ring | 2004

1.3 X 1.3 CM
18-karat yellow gold, 18-karat white gold,
yellow sapphire; fabricated, chased

PHOTO BY WALKER MONTGOMERY

Elizabeth Gualtieri and Jack Gualtieri

Renee Ring | 2002

1.2 X 2 CM

22-karat yellow gold, 18-karat yellow gold,
diamond, rubies, sapphires, tsavorite garnets;
hand fabricated, granulation, filigree, set

PHOTO BY DANIEL VAN ROSSEN
PRIVATE COLLECTION

Catherine Mannheim

Wedding and Engagement Rings | 2003

AVERAGE, 2 X 2 X 0.5 CM

Sapphire, ruby, diamond, white gold; cast

PHOTO BY FXP PHOTOGRAPHY

THE TEXT *reads: Once upon a time in a land far, far away, there lived a beautiful princess. The handsome Prince Charming rode upon his white horse, carried her off, and they lived happily ever after. Using this text as the form and structure of a wedding band in a way "unveils" the idealized story many women tell themselves about marriage and, consciously or not, project onto their own wedding rings.* —ADK

Alyssa Dee Krauss
Once Upon a Time... | 1996

1.8 X 1.8 X 0.3 CM
18-karat gold

PHOTO BY ARTIST

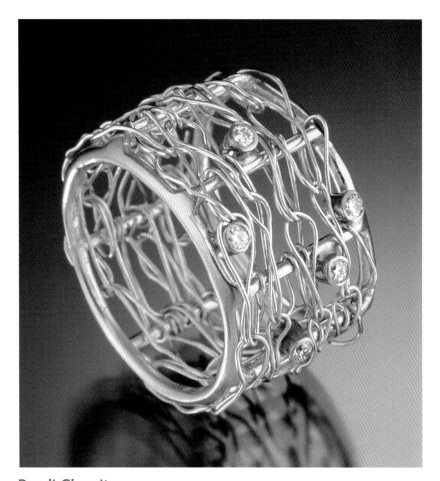

Randi Chervitz

18K Bamboo Ring with
5 Diamonds | 2005

2.2 X 1.3 X 2.2 CM
18-karat gold, diamonds; fabricated,
tube set, crocheted

PHOTO BY HAP SAKWA

Barbara Cohen

Tying the Knot | 2004

5 X 4 X 4 CM

18-karat gold, cultured pearl,
nylon mesh; fabricated

PHOTO BY THOMAS BRUKBAUER

Eva Franceschini

Continuita | 2006

EACH, 1.8 X 1.8 X 1 CM
18-karat gold, harmonic steel

PHOTO BY MARTINA ZANCAN
PRIVATE COLLECTION

Wendy Hacker-Moss

Golden Bloom | 2006

3 X 3.5 X 2 CM
Stainless steel mesh, 24-karat gold,
freshwater pearls, sterling silver,
metal clay; origami, fabricated

PHOTO BY SKIP BOLAN

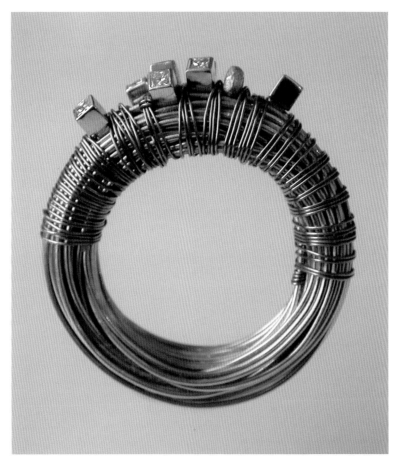

Jane Bowden

I'm Wrapped in You! | 2005

3.2 X 2.9 X 0.8 CM

18-karat yellow gold, 18-karat white gold, princess-cut diamonds

PHOTOS BY ARTIST

A **PERFECT** *blend of heaven and earth— my meteorite rings are unique, durable, and extremely comfortable. The anticlastic lining and edges create a wonderful comfort fit. The natural beauty of the meteorite is enhanced by etching.* —CP

Chris Ploof
Meteorite Ring | 2006

2.3 X 2.3 X 0.6 CM
Gibeon meteorite, 18-karat yellow gold;
forged, fabricated, etched

PHOTO BY ROBERT DIAMANTE

Lisa Ceccorulli

Untitled | 2006

EACH, 1.2 X 0.1 CM
Sterling silver, 22-karat gold; textured,
fused, hand fabricated, oxidized

PHOTO BY ALLAN CARLISLE

Barbara Paganin
Radiolari | 1992

3 X 3 X 1.5 CM
18-karat gold, silver,
diamonds; niello

PHOTOS BY ARTIST

Tim Carpenter
Untitled | 2006

2.5 X 2.5 X 0.8 CM
Tungsten carbide; machined

PHOTO BY ARTIST

Michelangelo Stanchi

Unione | 2006

LEFT, 6.5 X 1.9 CM;
RIGHT, 5.5 X 1.9 CM

14-karat white gold;
polished, brush finished

PHOTO BY ROBERT RAILY
COURTESY OF DOLCE SALINAS, SANTA FE, NEW MEXICO

Hisako Tsukamoto

Heat Sink | 2006

LEFT, 2 X 2 X 0.9 CM;
RIGHT, 2.4 X 2.4 X 0.9 CM

Titanium; machined

PHOTO BY ARTIST

Eun Mi Kim

Tension and Attention | 2003

EACH, 2.5 X 3.5 X 3.5 CM

Sterling silver, nylon; soldered,
hand fabricated

PHOTO BY MYUNG WOOK HUH

Ji Hoon Choi

Eternal | 2003

2.2 X 2.2 X 1 CM

Titanium, cubic zirconia; tension set

PHOTO BY KWANG CHOON PARK, KC STUDIO

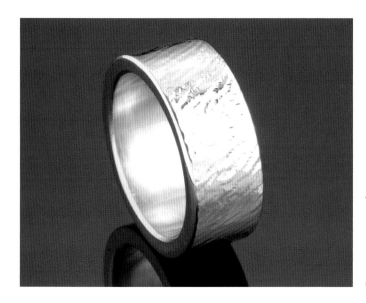

Timothy Meier

Water Band | 2006

2.5 X 2.5 X 1 CM
Stainless steel; lathe turned

PHOTO BY MATTHEW MEIER

Marisa Adamson

Vim | 2006

2.6 X 3.4 X 3 CM
Platinum Valley agate, diamonds,
14-karat palladium gold; cast

PHOTO BY BLASER PHOTOGRAPHY
COURTESY OF GOLDSMITH SILVERSMITH, INC.,
OMAHA, NEBRASKA

Hsia-Man Lydia Wang

Untitled | 2005

2.5 X 2.5 X 0.5 CM
Rough diamond, 14-karat white gold,
Damascus steel; fabricated

PHOTO BY ARTIST

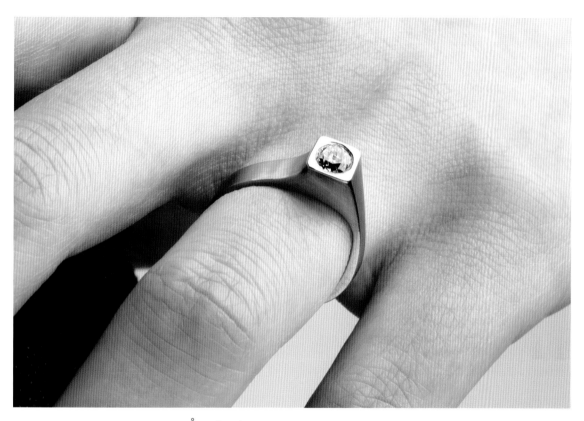

Åsa Lockner

My Favorite Wedding Ring | 2007

2 X 2.5 X 0.5 CM

White gold, coffee diamond; handwrought

PHOTOS BY MATS HÅKANSON

THE DOTS *on the ring spell "love" in Braille.* —MA

Maru Almeida
Love Is Blind | 2006

LARGEST, 0.8 X 2.2 X 2.2 CM

14-karat white gold, 14-karat yellow gold; hand carved, cast, fabricated

PHOTO BY ARTIST

Salima Thakker
Dancing Queen Collection | 2004

2.5 X 0.9 X 0.4 CM

18-karat gold; modular beadwork

PHOTO BY ARTIST

Jeannie Hwang

Missing Piece Ring | 2006

2.3 X 0.7 X 0.2 CM

18-karat palladium white gold,
sapphire, diamond baguettes

PHOTO BY HAP SAKWA

Philippe Tournaire
Tanaüs Ring | 2005

2.5 X 0.5 X 0.2 CM
Platinum, diamonds

PHOTO BY ARTIST

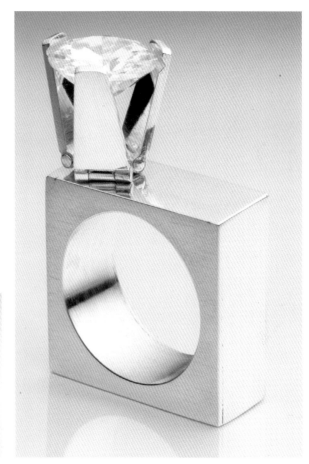

Hana Paik

Adjustable Ring | 2006

3.2 X 2 X 1.1 CM
Sterling silver, cubic zirconium; fabricated

PHOTOS BY KIM, SUNG-TAE

Ivan Sagel

Equality Joined | 2006

2.5 X 2.5 X 1 CM

Argentium silver, 18-karat gold, stainless steel,
diamonds; hand fabricated, assembled, bezel set

PHOTO BY GUY NICOL

James Kaya

Future | 2005

1.7 X 1.7 CM
Platinum, diamonds; tension set

PHOTOS BY ROBERT DIAMANTE

IN RECYCLED, *old wedding bands represent the past, the present, and the future. The one representing the past is an engraved band cast in resin to perfectly preserve it in time. In the band representing the present, the engraving has been removed and the ring polished, making it as good as new and ready to be worn again. The last ring is a container that holds a grain of gold made from a melted old band. The grain represents the possibilities of the future.* —CG

Christine Gaudernack

Recycled (Past, Present, and Future) | 2004

LEFT, 3.8 X 3 X 1.5 CM; CENTER, 2.2 X 2.2 X 0.6 CM; RIGHT, 3.6 X 2.8 X 1.5 CM
14-karat yellow gold, sterling silver, resin; cast, etched, oxidized

PHOTOS BY ARTIST

Claudia Stebler

Let's Melt Together | 2004

2.4 X 8 X 4.2 CM
Fine gold, fine silver, copper,
wood, magnets

PHOTOS BY PETRA JASCHKE

THE WOODEN *box closes magically with hidden magnets. Inside the two golden boxes are engagement rings out of thin silver strips, where you can imprint a message. The copper plates tell you what to do when you get married: Lass uns verschmelzen—Let's Melt Together. The metal is cast into a hand-carved charcoal form. Both rings are made in the same moment.* —CS

CREATING AN *engagement ring of ridiculous size gives it a weight that holds the wearer down or imitates the obsession with materiality.* —LBM

Lauren B. McAdams
Now, That's a Rock | 2006

32.5 X 20 X 11.3 CM
Steel, glass; gas welded, fabricated

PHOTO BY ARTIST

Tony P. Esola

Wedding Band | 2006

RING, 3 X 2 X 1 CM;
LOCK, 1.8 X 1.2 X 0.7 CM

Steel, 14-karat gold, stainless steel,
diamond; forged, cast, flush set

PHOTOS BY ARTIST

ATTACHED IS *a tongue-in-cheek commentary on modern views of relationships, marriage, and commitment. The history of the wedding ring is a symbol of fidelity, but what happens when there are more than two rings with Velcro? —GV*

Georgia Vandewater
Attached | 2005

LEFT, 2 X 1.5 X 0.6 CM; RIGHT, 2.3 X 2 X 0.1 CM
18-karat yellow gold, Velcro; cast, fabricated

PHOTO BY ARTIST

Hsueh-Ying Wu

Infinite Loop | 2006

2.5 X 3.5 X 4.5 CM

Plastic tube, stainless steel string;
hand fabricated

PHOTOS BY CHIN-TING CHIU

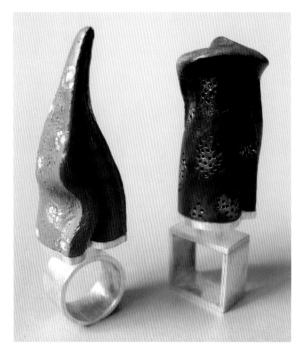

Hu Jun

Untitled | 2006

8 X 2.5 X 1 CM
Silver, resin, acrylic
color; soldered

PHOTO BY ARTIST
PRIVATE COLLECTION

Hui-Mei Pan

I Am Ready | 2004

3.4 X 2.7 X 2.7 CM
Sterling silver, 14-karat yellow gold,
crystal, peridot, coral; fabricated

PHOTO BY ARTIST

Azusa Fukawa

Turu/Creeper

4 X 8 X 0.9 CM
Sterling silver, 18-karat gold, copper, textile, enamel

PHOTOS BY ANDREAS ZIPPERLE

Simone Nolden

2 Worn | 2006

2.5 X 2 X 1 CM
9-karat gold, 18-karat gold, ruby; mounted, set

PHOTO BY ARTIST

Tanya Lyons
Handle with Care | 2007
LEFT, 3 X 3 X 0.8 CM; RIGHT, 2.8 X 2.8 X 0.8 CM
Glass; blown, cut, carved

PHOTO BY ARTIST

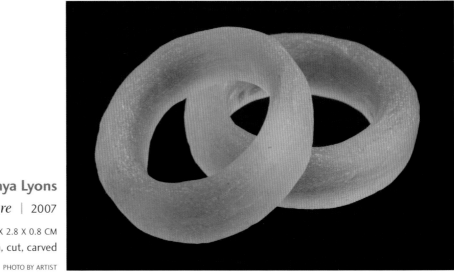

THESE GOLD *pills are meant to be ritually drunk with a glass of vodka by the bride and groom. They swallow this token of love as the most intimate gesture to celebrate their bond. Sadly, the owners abstained from the idea and bought themselves a pair of standard wedding rings. It's hard to break old habits, even at such a unique and personal occasion. The work remained a conceptual piece after all.* —TN

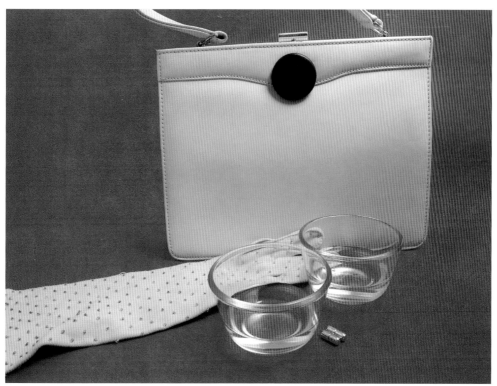

Ted Noten
Alternate for Wedding Ring 1 | 1997

EACH, 1.6 X 0.7 CM

24-karat gold; laser engraved

PHOTOS BY ARTIST
COLLECTION OF THE STEDELIJK MUSEUM,
AMSTERDAM, NETHERLANDS

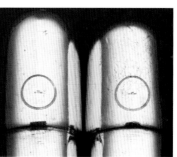

Gerd Rothmann

Fingerprint Wedding Rings | 2004

EACH, 0.8 X 2.1 X 2.2 CM
18-karat white gold; cast, fabricated

PHOTO BY STEFAN FRIEDEMANN
COURTESY OF ORNAMENTUM GALLERY, HUDSON, NEW YORK

THE PICTURE *shows the rings on the hands of the* *designers, who are husband and wife.* —VV & AF

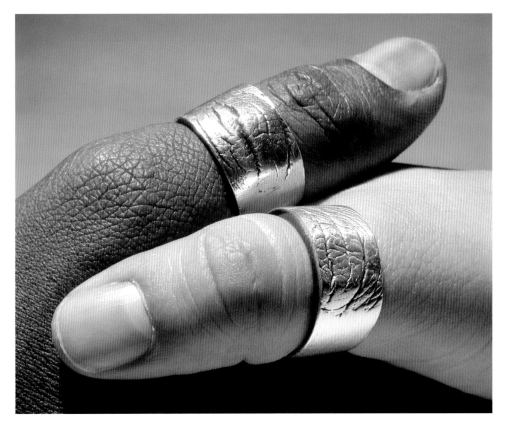

Valeria Vallarta and Alcides Fortes

Commitment Rings | 2000

1 X 2 X 2 CM
Silver; finger print transfer, cast

PHOTO BY EUGENIO BAÑUELOS

Hsi-Hsia Yang
Words in the Rings | 2005

3 X 14 X 39 CM
Silver, beeswax; cast, fabricated

PHOTO BY ARTIST

WEDDING RINGS *with personal handwriting. The signature is eternalized on the ring: a promise you wear every day.* —AL

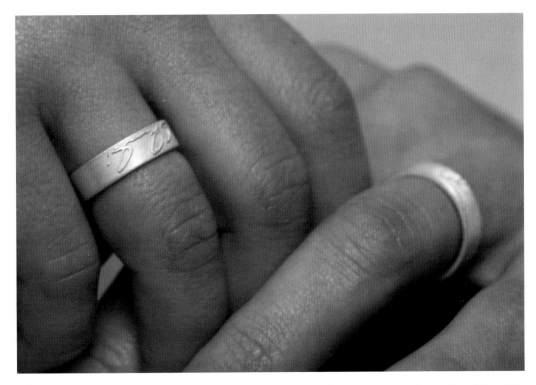

Alexa Lethen
Untitled | 2006

VARIABLE DIMENSIONS
Silver; 3D wax print, cast

PHOTOS BY ARTIST

Hsi-Hsia Yang

*Together Forever: Flower in a Mirror
or The Moon in the Water* | 2005

2.5 X 3 X 3 CM
Silver; cast, fabricated

PHOTO BY ARTIST

Eunyoung Park

Secret Love | 2006

2 X 2 X 1.2 CM
Sterling silver; cast

PHOTO BY ARTIST

THESE RINGS *are made using the handprints of the couple to be wedded. The model is made of soft wax so that the maximum amount of detail can be obtained. Giving their identity to one another, the couple exchanges something even more personal and unique than their name. Thus, the usual inner inscription on the wedding ring is replaced.* —MBE

Marta Boino Eliseu

Love Imprints | 2006

LEFT, 1.5 X 2 X 1.5 CM; RIGHT, 1 X 1.5 X 1 CM

Fine silver; lost wax cast

PHOTO BY ARTIST
COLLECTION OF ULLI REHM AND THOMAS DILL

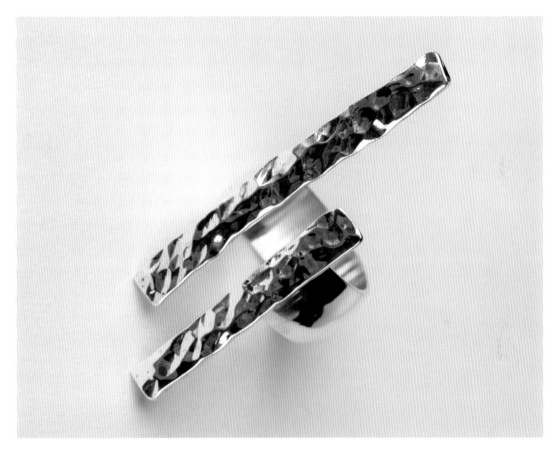

Marisa Adamson

Our Parallel Difference | 2005

2.2 X 2.1 X 5.1 CM
Sterling silver; constructed

PHOTO BY BLASER PHOTOGRAPHY
COURTESY OF GOLDSMITH SILVERSMITH, INC., OMAHA, NEBRASKA

Coconut Lu

Untitled | 2006

EACH, 1 X 2 X 2 CM
Sterling silver

PHOTOS BY ARTIST

EACH RING *is cast from a piece of stitched fabric. Leaving the white cast skin perfects the transposition from fabric into silver and causes confusion at first glance. Through wear, the cast skin changes slightly, giving it an unique shining silver patina. By this transformation through wear, the ring is an allegory for the development of love from untouched virginity to the beauty of experience.* —VS

Verena Schreppel
Gefasst | 2004

0.8 X 2.1 X 2.1 CM
Fabric, silver; sewn, cast

PHOTO BY ARTIST

Daphne van der Meulen
Felt Ring | 2006

0.2 X 2 X 2 CM
10-karat yellow gold,
sterling silver; cast

PHOTO BY ARTIST

THE LENGTH *of the gold thread corresponds to the bride and groom's measurements from head to toe.* —MT

Marcus Teipel
From Head to Toe | 2006
LEFT, 2.7 X 0.6 CM; RIGHT, 2.3 X 0.6 CM
White gold
PHOTO BY OLGA PLANAS

Nikolay Sardamov

Rings, Opposites' Attraction | 2007

LEFT, 2.6 X 2.5 X 2.5 CM; RIGHT, 1.2 X 2.3 X 2.3 CM

18-karat gold, sterling silver

PHOTO BY ANGEL PENCHEV

Hsueh-Ying Wu

Wedding Gauze | 2006

AVERAGE, 3.1 X 2.8 X 1 CM

Sterling silver, copper, stainless steel mesh;
hand fabricated

PHOTO BY CHIN-TING CHIU

Mitsue Slattery
Untitled | 2005

0.7 X 2.5 CM
18-karat yellow gold

PHOTO BY ARTIST

DOUBLE HAPPINESS *often appears in Chinese traditional arts and crafts, especially in paper-cut art. This logo means happiness, marriage, fruitfulness, and more.* —HJ

Hu Jun
Double Happiness | 2006

10.5 X 10 X 0.5 CM
Silver; carved, soldered

PHOTO BY ARTIST
PRIVATE COLLECTION

Micha Yehieli

Untitled | 2006

2.5 X 1.8 X 1.7 CM
22-karat gold, platinum; hand fabricated

PHOTO BY ALEXANDER KUCHERENK

Stefano Marchetti

Untitled | 1995

2.3 X 2.3 X 0.6 CM
Gold, silver; mokume parquetry

PHOTO BY ARTIST

Ilana Rabinovich-Slonim

Yehudit's Rings | 2003

TOP, 1.3 X 2.5 X 2.5 CM
18-karat gold; hand fabricated,
carved, cast

PHOTOS BY SHLOMI BERNTHAL

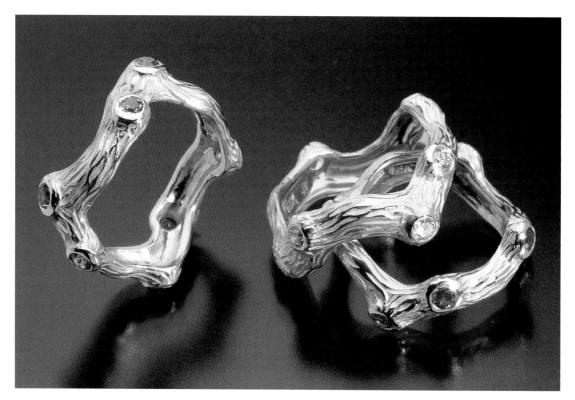

Julia Fluker

Vine Rings | 2002

EACH, 2 X 2 X 0.4 CM
18-karat gold, green sapphires,
diamonds, blue sapphires; cast

PHOTO BY DOUG YAPLE

Dahlia Kanner

Pod Ring with Branchy Band | 2000

1.2 X 0.3 X 0.5 CM
18-karat gold, diamonds; cast

PHOTO BY MARK JOHNSON

Cynthia Eid

Two Become One | 1979

2.5 X 2.5 X 1.3 CM
18-karat yellow gold; forged

PHOTOS BY ARTIST

Hannah Louise Lamb
Two Part Rings | 2006

DEPTH, 0.6 CM
18-karat gold, silver

PHOTO BY ARTIST

Dayna M. Orione-Kim

Untitled | 2005

2.5 X 2 X 1.3 CM

18-karat gold, yellow beryl;
hand fabricated, repoussé

PHOTO BY ALAN FARKAS

Cesar Lim and Vlad Lavrovsky

Fringed Wedding Bands | 2006

2 X 2 X 4 CM

18-karat gold, diamonds; hand
fabricated, textured, collet set

PHOTO BY ARTIST

Christopher A. Hentz

Untitled | 1989

1.9 X 1.5 X 1 CM

14-karat yellow gold, diamonds,
andalusite; fabricated

PHOTO BY RALPH GABRINER

So Young Park
Untitled | 2006

2 X 2 X 0.5 CM

18-karat yellow gold, diamonds; hammered, soldered, hand fabricated, set

PHOTO BY MUNCH STUDIO

Kari Rinn
Flax Embrace | 2005

1 X 1.5 X 1.5 CM

Palladium, 14-karat green gold; cast

PHOTO BY TAYLOR DABNEY

MODULAR GOLDEN *beads are inserted. The ring looks solid but feels soft and playful.* —ST

Salima Thakker
Dancing Queen Collection | 2004

2.5 X 0.9 X 0.4 CM
18-karat yellow gold; modular beadwork

PHOTO BY ARTIST

Stephen Kris
2 Become 1 | 2005

2.5 X 1 CM
18-karat yellow gold, diamond;
fabricated, formed

PHOTO BY RALPH GABRINER

Matthieu Cheminée

Nothing Is Lost, All Is Found | 2006

2.3 X 0.8 X 2.3 CM

18-karat gold, found rusted metal,
citrine, diamonds; hand stamped

PHOTOS BY ANTHONY MCLEAN

THROUGH FIRE *and force, a single element is created. It is then divided into two and each evolves along its own path. Each reflects similarities with the other, yet is distinct and whole unto itself.* —KJ

Kelly Johnson

Forged Pair | 2006

LEFT, 2.5 X 1.4 X 2.5 CM; RIGHT, 1.9 X 1.3 X 1.9 CM

18-karat yellow gold, 14-karat yellow gold, sterling silver; fused, forged, etched

PHOTO BY GEORGE POST

Pam Robinson

Untitled | 2006

TOP, 2.5 X 0.5 CM; BOTTOM, 2.6 X 0.9 CM

14-karat yellow gold, sterling silver,
diamond; hand fabricated, hollow
formed, textured, flush set

PHOTO BY CINDY TRIM

Federico Vianello

Flat and Half-Round Wedding Files | 2006

EACH, 2.3 X 0.9 X 2.3 CM
18-karat yellow gold, 18-karat
red gold, steel files

PHOTO BY DUILIO RINGRESSI

THESE RINGS *were made from a pair of antique Swedish nails I received as a gift. They were found in an old ore mine north of the Arctic Circle and are probably more than 100 years old. They were used for the surface texture that developed over time from use and exposure to the elements.* —RJ

Rob Jackson
Nail Wedding Rings | 2002

LEFT, 2.5 X 2.3 X 0.7 CM;
RIGHT, 2.3 X 2.1 X 0.7 CM

Iron, faceted oval diamond, black diamonds, natural diamond crystal; fabricated, bezel set, tube set

PHOTO BY ARTIST

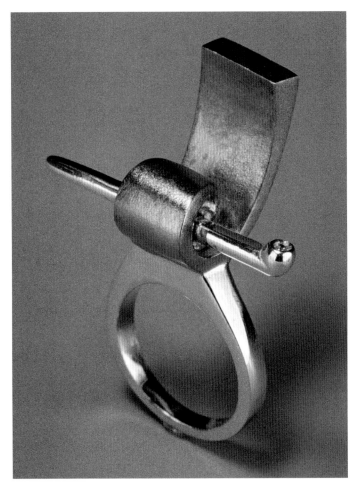

IN KOREAN *culture,*
they say "raising hair"
as a metaphor for a
wedding. I want to express
a mature bride with an
ornamental hair-pin in her
black hair. —HDW

Han Dong Won
Being a Woman | 2006

3.8 X 3 X 1.8 CM
14-karat yellow gold, diamond;
wax worked, cast, black plated

PHOTO BY NA ILKYU

Jason Morrissey

Damascus Steel Bands | 2007

TOP, 2.1 X 2.1 CM; BOTTOM, 1.7 X 1.7 CM

Steel; layered, forge welded,
twisted, carved

PHOTO BY ROBERT DIAMANTE

Maya Kini

Ceremonial Markings 2 | 2006

0.8 X 3 X 3 CM
Graphite; carved, machined

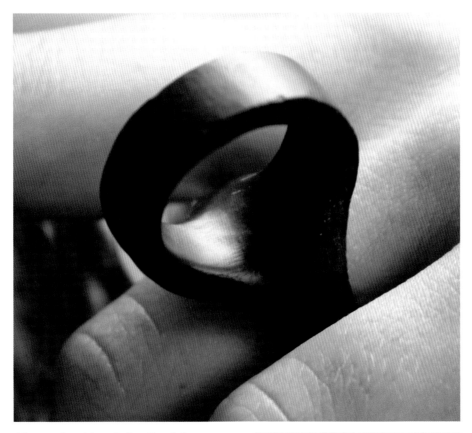

Alexandra Martinho Rodrigues

Untitled | 2006

4.2 X 2.4 X 1.8 CM
Basalt; lapidary

PHOTOS BY MARIA MIRE

PEOPLE LIKE *to marry, but some of them can't stand to wear a ring* —TN

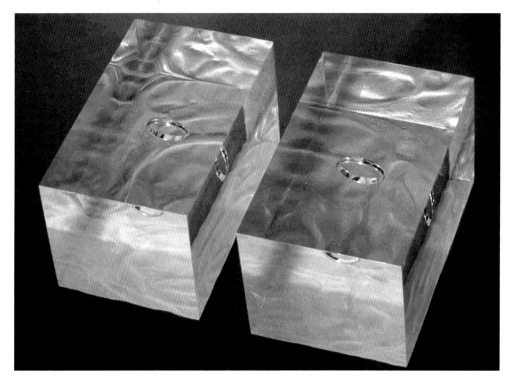

Ted Noten

Alternative for Wedding Rings 3 | 1997

EACH CUBE, 7 X 7 X 11 CM

Wedding rings, acrylic; cast

PHOTO BY ARTIST
PRIVATE COLLECTION

Christine J. Brandt

Desiree | 2006

6 X 3 X 3.5 CM

African black ebony,
Herkimer diamond clusters;
hand carved, set

PHOTO BY MICHAEL BRANDT

Reneé Zettle-Sterling
Cherished Rings, Cherished Earth | 2006

LEFT, 3.8 X 3.2 X 1.3 CM; RIGHT, 3.2 X 3.2 X 1.3 CM
Compressed earth; cut

PHOTO BY ARTIST

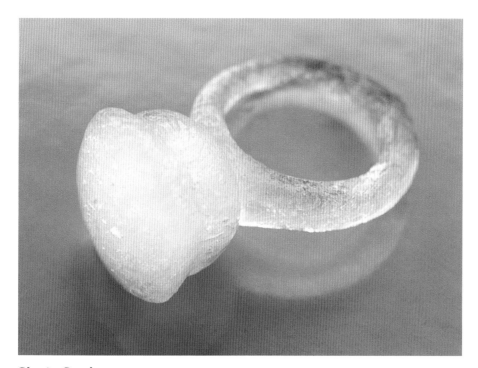

Glynis Gardner

Love You Long Time | 2007

5 X 3.5 X 3 CM
Ice

PHOTO BY JAMES KIRK

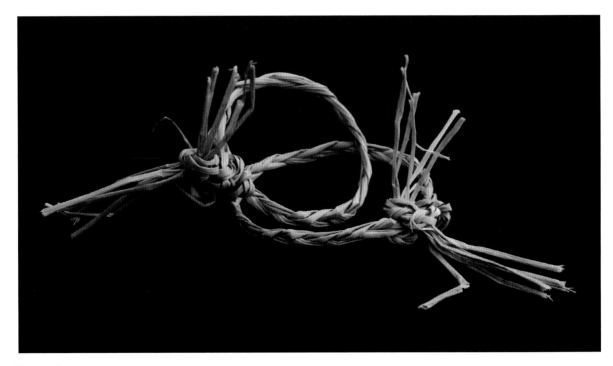

Tanya Lyons

Growth | 2006

LEFT, 4 X 2.2 X 3; RIGHT, 4 X 2 X 3.3 CM
Grass; braided

PHOTO BY ARTIST

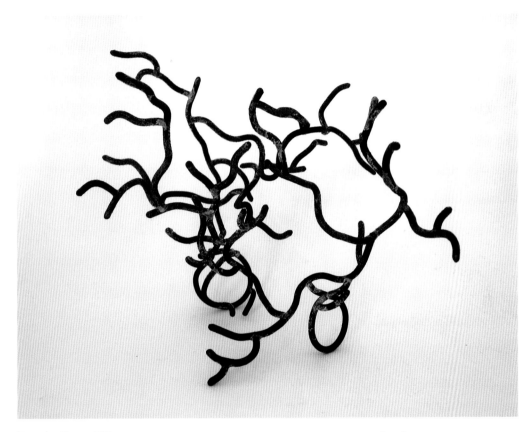

Estela Saez Vilanova

My Wedding Rings | 2006

11 X 15 X 10 CM

Iron

PHOTO BY ARTIST

BECAUSE HE *is mine now*
Because he is me and I am him
Because my roots and his roots will become one
Because this is forever
Because I love him. —ESV

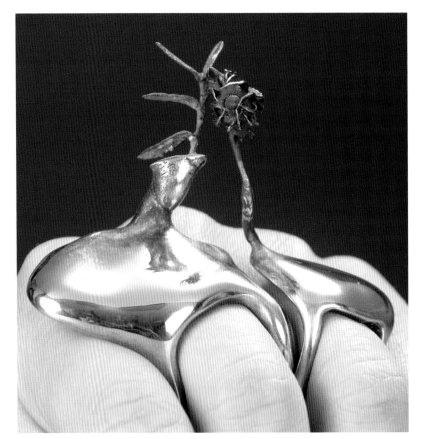

Chiu Hui-Yu

Yes, I Do!! | 2007

Bronze, ready-made object; cast

PHOTOS BY ARTIST
PRIVATE COLLECTION

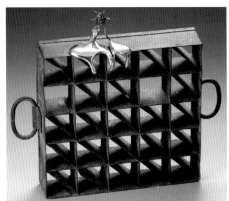

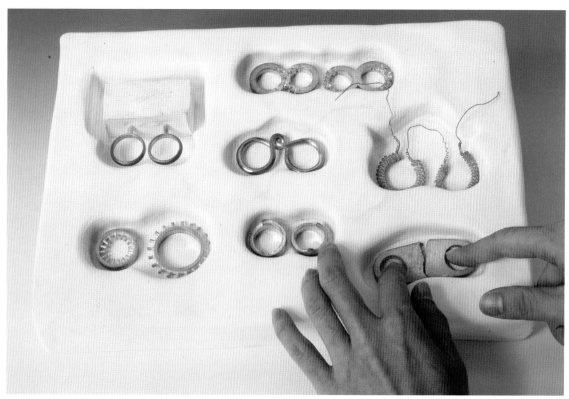

Hsi-Hsia Yang
Contract | 2005

4 X 32 X 26 CM

Silver, plaster; cast, fabricated

PHOTOS BY ARTIST

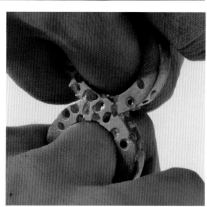

Sora Maruyama
From Mother Earth | 2005

LARGEST, 2.5 X 2.5 X 1.2 CM
Yakusugi (cedar), platinum

PHOTO BY ARTIST

MY LIFELONG *fascination and study of fairy tales, folklore, ancient religion, and myth is a major influence in my artwork. In "Bluebeard's Tale," a young bride is given the keys to her husband's castle and told to enjoy searching all its rooms and the vast riches it holds— except for one small room in the dungeon. His bride and her sisters are driven crazy with curiosity until, unable to stand it any longer, they unlock the secret door and discover the dismembered corpses of Bluebeard's ex-wives. Sometimes in the creative journey I discover insights about myself or my subject matter that reveal truths that I would rather not know. But that is what makes the artist's life a heroic and interesting journey.* —SR

Shona Rae

Bluebeard's Wedding Rings | 2007

TOTAL, 12 X 10.5 X 4.8 CM
Bone, sterling silver, beeswax; carved, pierced, constructed, painted

PHOTO BY ARTIST

Shelby Ferris Fitzpatrick
Domesticity Wedding Rings | *2005*

EACH, 5 X 4.4 X 4.4 CM
Silver, silk; spun, fabricated, laser etched

PHOTOS BY MIKE BLISSETT
PRIVATE COLLECTION

Sarah Doremus

Fur Lined Wedding Rings | 2005

EACH, 9 X 1 X 9 CM
Sterling silver, copper, rabbit fur

PHOTO BY DEAN POWELL

Yoshie Hattori

Four Pearl Ring | 2006

3 X 3.5 X 3.5 CM
Coated wire, pearls, silver; crocheted

PHOTO BY ARTIST

Ami Avellán

Sounds Like Just Married | 2006

LEFT, 10 X 6 CM; RIGHT, 9 X 5 CM
Sterling silver, linen thread, freshwater pearls; cast

PHOTO BY ARTIST

141

THE MATERIAL *that I predominantly use is a finely woven stainless steel mesh. Large sheets are cut into squares and folded, origami style, into small flower-like forms. Through the process of simply folding the material several times, it goes from a flimsy, lifeless format to one of vibrancy, sturdiness and resiliency.* —WHM

Wendy Hacker-Moss
"She Loves Me" Blossom Ring | 2007

3.5 X 4 X 2.5 CM
Stainless steel mesh, sterling silver, garnets;
origami, hand folded, woven

PHOTO BY ED IKUTA

INSTEAD OF *roses, a man can propose with this ring, which looks like a full bloom when worn. The ring then serves as a wearable bridal bouquet at the wedding.* —CHK

Chao-Hsien Kuo
Lumipallo | 2005

5.5 X 8 X 9 CM
Sterling silver; anticlastic formed

PHOTOS BY ARTIST

Koldodesign

White Gold with Aquamarine | 2006

2.7 X 2.2 X 2.1 CM
White gold, aquamarine; cast, set, finished

PHOTOS BY KOLDODESIGN

Gurhan

Eternity Rose-Cut Diamond Ring | 2006

2.5 X 2.5 X 0.6 CM

Platinum, white and champagne rose-cut
diamonds; hand fabricated

PHOTO BY RALPH GABRINER

Marc Stiglitz

Circle of Life & Love Engagement Ring and Wedding Band Set | 2006

LEFT, 2.3 X 0.5 X 2 CM; RIGHT, 2.1 X 0.4 X 2 CM

Platinum, Ideal-cut diamond, brilliant-cut diamonds, princess-cut diamonds; lost wax cast, channel set, prong set, pavé set

PHOTO BY GEORGE POST PHOTOGRAPHY

Lazare Kaplan International, Inc.

The Lazare Diamond Platinum Pavé Twist Band | 2005

Platinum, ideal-cut diamonds; micro-pavé set

PHOTO BY DARREN ROSARIO

Jan Mandel

Ewa's Ring | 2003

2 X 2 CM

18-karat white gold, diamond;
hand fabricated, constructed

PHOTOS BY FXP PHOTOGRAPHY

THERE IS *a saying that if a woman's engagement ring fits on the man's pinky finger, they were meant to be. This ring is meant to fit on the same finger for both female and male.* —JY

Jeong Youn

A Ring For Him AND Her | 2006

LEFT, 1.5 X 1.8 X 2 CM; RIGHT 1.8 X 2 X 2.2 CM
Fine silver; hand fabricated, cast

PHOTO BY PAUL NURNBERG

Wen Liueh Kueh

Purity | 2006

3.7 X 2.2 X 3.5 CM
Sterling silver, freshwater pearl;
hand fabricated

PHOTO BY VICKY LAM

Hea Jin Yang
1+1=1 | 2006

3.4 X 5 X 2 CM
Sterling silver; hand fabricated

PHOTOS BY KWANG CHOON PARK, KC STUDIO

Hratch Babikian

Burns Engagement | 2006

2.5 X 1.5 X 2.5 CM

Palladium, diamonds; carved,
cast, forged, fabricated

PHOTOS BY ARTIST
COLLECTION OF CHRISTOPHER AND LYNNE BURNS

Karin Jacobson

*Square Solitaire and
Square Wedding Band* | 2006

BAND, 0.4 X 0.2 CM; SOLITAIRE, 0.4 X 0.6 CM
Palladium, moissanite; cast,
bezel set, flush set

PHOTO BY SEAN TUBRIDY

Hans Stofer

*Finger Nail – Engagement
Signet Ring* | 2002

3 X 3 CM
Mild steel nail; engraved

PHOTO BY ARTIST
COURTESY OF THE ALICE AND LOUIS KOCH COLLECTION,
BASEL, SWITZERLAND

Li-Sheng Cheng
Untitled | 2005

1.5 X 2 X 2 CM
Silver, pearls; fabricated

PHOTO BY ARTIST

Michael Dean
Sunset | 2000

2.5 X 2 X 1.1 CM
Japanese pink button pearl, 18-karat gold,
blue diamonds, platinum; forged

PHOTO BY DIAMONDDON

COURTESY OF THE MICHAEL DEAN DESIGN GALLERY,
VANCOUVER, BRITISH COLUMBIA, CANADA

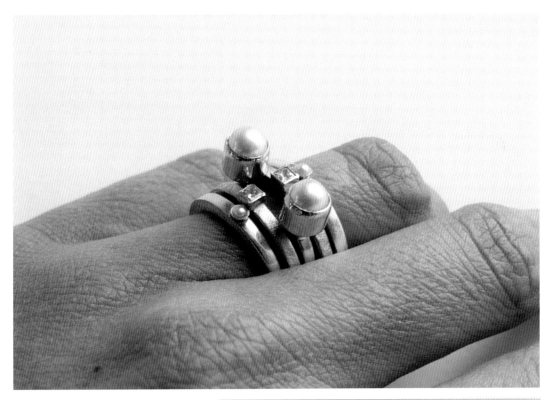

Keri Ataumbi

Pearl Bowl, Pearl Bar and Pearl Stirrup Rings | 2006

LEFT, 2 X 3 X 1 CM; CENTER, 2 X 2.5 X 1 CM; RIGHT, 2 X 3 X 0.5 CM

14-karat gold, Akoya pearls; fabricated

PHOTOS BY ARTIST

THE BIEDERMEIER *design movement was the forerunner to Destijl and Bauhaus. It was founded on the concept of elegance of line and refinement of form to its essential elements.* —NA

Nanz Aalund

Biedermeier Engagement | 2003

2.6 X 0.8 X 2.6 CM
Platinum, 18-karat yellow gold,
diamond; fabricated

PHOTO BY JIM FORBES

IF HER *heart needs a little warming, give her* Melting Glacier. —LJ

Lezlie Jane

Melting Glacier | 2005

4.2 X 2.8 X 3.5 CM

14-karat white gold, ice blue topaz, moonstones, diamonds

PHOTO BY DOUG YAPLE

Eddie Sakamoto

Untitled | 1996

2.3 X 2 X 0.8 CM

18-karat yellow gold, platinum,
diamonds; hand fabricated

PHOTO BY ARTIST

Eddie Sakamoto

Untitled | 2001

2.5 X 2.1 X 1.2 CM

Platinum, 18-karat yellow gold,
white and canary diamonds; cast

PHOTO BY ARTIST

Esther Davies

Untitled | 2002

5.1 X 3.8 X 3.8 CM
Sterling silver, 18-karat gold,
cubic zirconia; hand fabricated

PHOTO BY HAP SAKWA

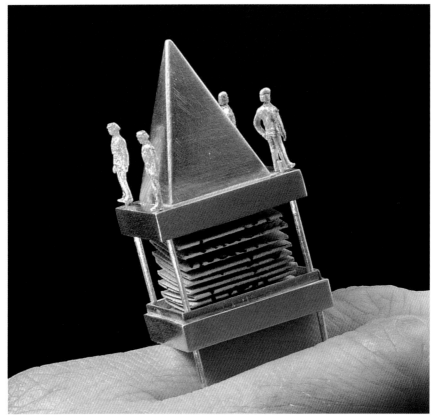

THIS WEDDING *ring can be opened and closed. When the ring is open, the piece of paper inside the ring is visible. The partner has written down on this paper why he or she wants to marry the other. The text is kept as a special treasure enclosed in the ring.* —IV

Ingeborg Vandamme
Wedding-Ring I | 1995

2.3 X 2.3 X 5.5 CM

Silver, paper; soldered, cast

PHOTOS BY HENNIE VAN BEEK
PRIVATE COLLECTION

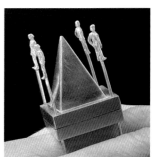

DAMASCUS STAINLESS *steel is a corrosion resistant and incredibly strong metal of legendary properties. Crusaders highly sought weapons made from Damascus steel because of its strength. My Damascus rings are perfectly suited for the modern "warrior" in all of us.* —CP

Chris Ploof
12_26 Angles Ring | 2005

2.4 X 2.4 X 0.6 CM

Damascus stainless steel, 18-karat yellow gold; forged, fabricated, lathe turned, milled, swaged, etched

PHOTO BY ROBERT DIAMANTE

Maureen Murphy
Untitled | 2005

3.5 X 2.5 X 2 CM

Sterling silver, cubic zirconia; hollow constructed

PHOTO BY ARTIST

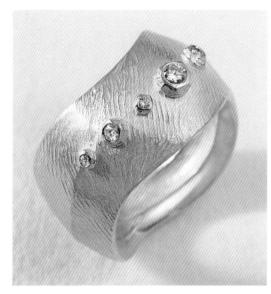

Dahlia Kanner

Mom's Ring | 2005

1.4 X 0.3 CM

18-karat gold, diamonds; cast

PHOTO BY CHARLES ESTABROOKS

Jan Daggett

Kite Shaped Diamond in 18-Karat Gold | 2001

2.3 X 2.1 X 1.1 CM

18-karat gold, diamonds; hard wax carved, lost wax cast, sandblasted

PHOTO BY ARTIST

THE MAGIC *of mokume gane, Japanese for "eye of the wood,"*
is that no two rings are ever the same. —WW

Wayne Werner
Mokume Gane Rings | 2006

2.5 X 2.5 X 0.6 CM
Silver, 14-karat palladium white gold,
18-karat yellow gold, 14-karat white gold,
platinum; mokume gane, hand forged

PHOTO BY RALPH GABRINER

Geoffrey D. Giles

Two Stripe Set | 2005

LARGER, 2.4 X 2.4 X 0.6 CM;
SMALLER, 2.1 X 2.1 X 0.4 CM

18-karat yellow gold, 18-karat palladium
white gold; married metal, fabricated,
brushed surface embellishments

PHOTO BY TAYLOR DABNEY

Todd Reed

Untitled | 2005

1.3 X 2.3 CM
18-karat yellow gold, diamond octahedrons,
diamond macles

PHOTO BY AZADPHOTO.COM

Stefano Marchetti

Untitled | 1995

2.3 X 2.6 X 0.8 CM
Gold, silver; mokume parquetry

PHOTO BY ROBERTO SORDI

Michael Zobel

Untitled | 2003

LARGER, 2 X 0.8 CM; SMALLER, 1.7 X 0.8 CM

Palladium, 22-karat gold, platinum, diamond baguette

PHOTO BY FRED THOMAS

Noam Elyashiv

Engagement Ring: Silhouette | 2000

2.4 X 2 X 0.8 CM

18-karat yellow gold, citrine, champagne
diamond; hollow constructed

PHOTO BY MARTIN DOYLE

Jeannie Hwang

Donut Bands | 2005

LEFT, 2.4 X 0.3 X 0.3 CM;
RIGHT, 2.1 X 0.2 X 0.2 CM

18-karat yellow gold,
18-karat white gold

PHOTO BY HAP SAKWA

Jill Newbrook

Untitled | 2006

0.9 X 2 CM

18-karat rose, yellow, and
white gold; fabricated

PHOTO BY JOËL DEGEN
COLLECTION OF DR. BENGI BEYZADE

Joan Tenenbaum

River Ring with Trillion Diamond | 2006

1.3 X 2 X 2 CM

18-karat gold, 22-karat gold, sterling silver,
diamond; mokume gane, hand fabricated, inlaid

PHOTO BY DOUG YAPLE

Andy Cooperman

Canyon Rings | 2004

EACH, 0.7 X 2.2 CM
14-karat white gold, 18-karat
yellow gold; cast, fabricated

PHOTO BY DOUG YAPLE

Nicole Jacquard

Wedding Ring Set | 2000

2.5 X 1.5 CM

18-karat yellow gold, diamonds,
sapphires; cast, granulation

PHOTOS BY KEVIN MONTAGUE

Kim Eric Lilot

Bound and Gagged
Wedding Band | 1997

0.4 X 0.9 X 2.5 CM

Platinum, 18-karat gold; fabricated,
twisted, soldered

PHOTO BY ARTIST

Tracy Johnson

Ribbon Band | 2004

2.5 X 0.7 CM

18-karat gold, 22-karat gold; fabricated

PHOTO BY ROBERT DIAMANTE

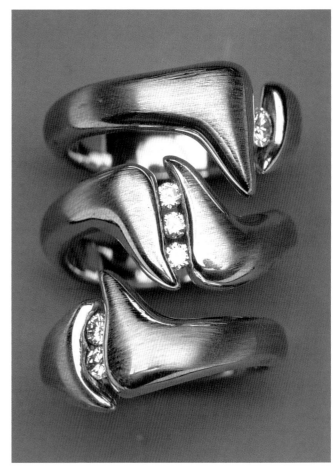

Kirk Lang
Untitled | 2000

EACH, 2 X 2 X 1 CM
18-karat white gold, diamonds

PHOTO BY ROBERT MULLER

Pamela Froman

Scroll Crush Wedding Set | 2006

LARGEST, 2 X 2 X 0.3 CM
18-karat white gold, diamonds;
crushed finish

PHOTO BY JAY LAWRENCE GOLDMAN

Yesim Yuksek

Gothic Bride + Deco Bride | 2006

TALLEST, 3.3 X 2.3 X 0.8 CM

Sterling silver, white cubic zirconia,
18-karat yellow gold; cast, hand fabricated,
soldered, constructed, bezel set

PHOTOS BY ADIL GUMUSOGLU
COURTESY ALEF GALERI, ISTANBUL, TURKEY

Tsvetelina Alexieva

Rings Endless Spiral I and II | 2006

EACH, 1.9 X 2.5 X 2.5 CM
18-karat gold, sterling silver

PHOTO BY ANGEL PENCHEV

I AM *interested in the concept of dissipative structure, the structure of self-renewal, of flowing balance. Each piece is a moment caught between movements.* —DD

Deborrah Daher

Bands | 2004

RIGHT, 1.5 X 1.5 CM

18-karat yellow gold, shibuishi, champagne and silver diamonds; fabricated, forged

PHOTO BY RALPH GABRINER

Alyssa Dee Krauss

The Ring That Binds Series:
The Book of Let Me Count the Ways | 2002

2 X 2 X 0.4 CM
18-karat gold

PHOTO BY KEVIN DOWNEY

WHEN MY *husband proposed, I felt he needed an engagement ring too. As a result, this ring has turned into my most popular wedding band for men and women. The iron is virtually indestructible, while the gold creates a perfect foil for its darkness.* —PF

Peg Fetter

Stuart's Engagement Ring | 2003

2 X 2 X 0.2 CM

Iron, 14-karat yellow gold; forged, fabricated

PHOTO BY DON CASPER

THE IDEA *for this piece was to turn around the traditional "eternal band" concept and suggest the forging of two parties, coming together as one.* —NB

Nick Grant Barnes

Touch | 2006

2 X 2 CM

Fine silver, 24-karat gold; fold formed, fabricated, soldered, overlaid

PHOTOS BY GREG STALEY

Fabrizio Tridenti

Sand Circles | 2006

2.5 X 2.2 X 0.6 CM
Oxidized silver, sand

PHOTO BY LUCIANO DI LELLO

Hsia-Man Lydia Wang

Untitled | 2005

2.5 X 2.5 X 0.5 CM
Ruby, 14-karat yellow gold, Damascus steel; fabricated

PHOTO BY ARTIST

Susan R. Ewing

Prague Star: Wedding Ring
for Jan Nepomuk | 1999

2.3 X 1.5 X 2.3 CM
18-karat gold, mild steel; fabricated

PHOTO BY JEFFREY SABO

Alexandra Martinho Rodrigues

Masculine? Feminine? | 2006

1.1 X 2.7 X 1.9 CM
Brass; gilded

PHOTOS BY MARIA MIRE

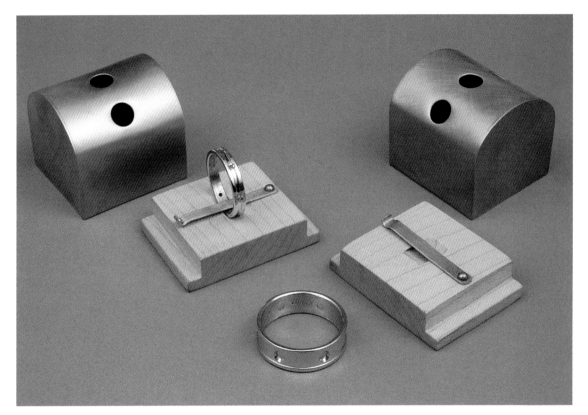

Christopher C. Darway

Untitled | 1998

6 X 7 X 6 CM
14-karat yellow gold, maple wood,
bronze; lost wax cast

PHOTO BY CHET BOLINS

THIS RING *is a humorous version of the traditional solitaire and created for those clients who are sensitive to using any stone associated with conflict.* —AK

Amanda Keidan
Diamond Silhouette Ring | 2006

2.5 X 2 X 0.4 CM
18-karat yellow gold; wax carved

PHOTO BY BERNARD WOLF

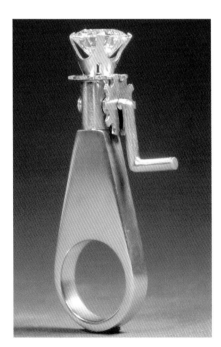

Cassandra L. Foral
Mine Is Bigger than Yours | 2006

6.4 X 2.5 CM
Silver, brass, cubic zirconia

PHOTO BY KATE BRENNAN

Fritz Maierhofer

Wedding Rings for Miek and Willem | 1993

LARGEST, 3 X 4 X 0.2 CM
White gold, yellow gold

PHOTO BY WILLEM VANDEKERCKHOVE

Peter Deckers

Wedding Award | 2001

2.9 X 0.5 X 1.9 CM

Sterling silver, 18-karat gold, gold
plate; pierced, fabricated

PHOTO BY ARTIST

Julie Brooks Price

Now We Check the Married Box | 2002

2 X 1.5 X 2.5 CM

Sterling silver, pre-enameled steel, enamel decals,
letraset decals, resin; fabricated

PHOTO BY ARTIST

THESE RINGS *are based on the book* The Little Prince *by Antoine de Saint-Exupéry. The little prince is responsible for the rose that grows on his planet. He protects her with glass from the winds and animals. When two people belong together, they are responsible for and very careful with each other.* —CL

Claudia Langer

You know...my flower, I am responsible for her!
(Antoine de Saint-Exupéry) | 1997

7.8 X 2.3 X 1.6 CM

Sterling silver, glass; sawed, bent, soldered

PHOTOS BY ARTIST
COURTESY OF THE KOCH COLLECTION, BASEL, SWITZERLAND

THE SWEETNESS *of*
commitment, guarded
and protected. —NB

Nina Basharova
Sugar and Barbed Wire Ring | 2006

3.2 X 1.8 X 1 CM
Sugar, sterling silver; hand fabricated,
oxidized, set

PHOTO BY BRYAN MCCAY

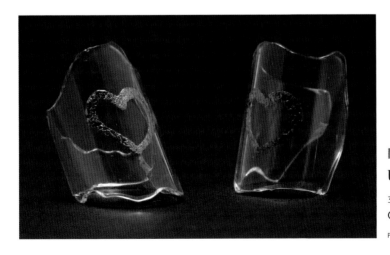

Niina Mahlberg
Untitled | 2006

3 X 1.8 X 1.8 CM
Glass, copper; lampworked

PHOTO BY RURIK MAHLBERG

MAGNETISM REPRESENTS *the sudden awakening to the new limitations of the committed lifestyle.* —KN

Karin Nir

Magnetism | 2006

1.8 X 0.4 X 2.2 CM

24-karat gold-plated brass, magnet, iron, paper; lathed, pressure impression

PHOTOS BY ARTIST

Azusa Fukawa

Match | 2005–2006

LEFT, 3.5 X 4 X 1.8 CM;
RIGHT, 4 X 2.5 X 2.2 CM

Sterling silver, citrine,
plastic, steel, garnet

PHOTOS BY MARTIN PECHLANER

Ami Avellán
Still Waiting | 2006

UPPER, 10 X 2.4 CM; LOWER, 8 X 2.1 CM
Sterling silver, sewing thread; cast

PHOTO BY ARTIST

IN MANY *cultures, the coin is related to good luck. This inspired us to make a wedding "coin" pendant to wear close to the heart. The magic words "love is all that matters" are engraved around the coin. More layers can be added, collecting the story of your life. When not worn, the coins remain visible in a special container, showing the message and colors on the side.* —AT & PB

Annette Tjho and Pauline Barendse
Good Luck Wedding Pendant | 2007

EACH, 5 X 2.5 X 2.5 CM

Sterling silver, 18-karat gold, aluminum, corian, titanium; anodized, photo transfer, cast, engraved, laser welded

PHOTOS BY ROB GLASTRA

Elisa Gulminelli

Marriage of Convenience/ Love for Money | 2006

EACH, 2.5 X 2.5 X 0.1 CM
Credit cards; fabricated

PHOTO BY ARTIST

Tessa Elizabeth Rickard

See No Evil, Hear No Evil, Speak No Evil Wedding Bands | 2006

EACH, 3.8 X 3 X 2.7 CM
Sterling silver, 14-karat yellow gold, plastic, cubic zirconia, alexandrite; fabricated, soldered

PHOTO BY TIM CARPENTER

Pia Schmalen
Untitled | 2004

2.7 X 2.7 X 1.1 CM

Marzipan, sugar icing,
sterling silver

PHOTO BY ARTIST

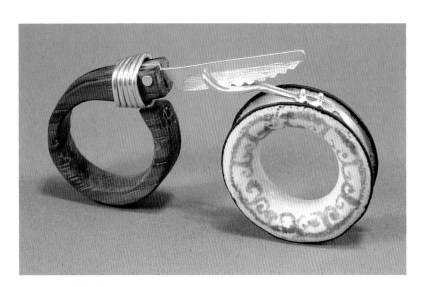

Vanessa Neily
He feeds me _____; She feeds me _____. | 2006

LEFT, 3 X 6 X 1 CM; RIGHT, 3 X 4 X 1 CM

Sterling silver, copper, padauk wood, enamel

PHOTO BY ARTIST

Annie Tung

Divorce Ring: A Broken Nest, a Broken Ring | 2005

EACH HALF, 3 X 3 X 2.8 CM
Sterling silver, patina; cast

PHOTO BY ARTIST

Joe Casey Doyle

His and His: Til Death Do Us Part | 2006

EACH, 3.5 X 5.5 X 4.5 CM
Sterling silver, steel, enamel; sifted, torch fired

PHOTO BY ARTIST

Kate Short

Godzilla Wedding Bands | 2000

EACH, 2.3 X 0.8 X 2.3 CM
18-karat white gold, action figure

PHOTO BY HAP SAKWA

Mark Kummeth

Til' Death | 2005

LEFT, 2.3 X 0.6 X 2.3 CM;
RIGHT, 2.5 X 1 X 2.5 CM

Sterling silver; cast

PHOTO BY ARTIST

FEW THINGS *are more inflated than the value of diamonds and the appeal of the traditional solitaire engagement setting. Maybe fate occasionally takes a hand in destroying them during the modern re-tipping process.* —MR

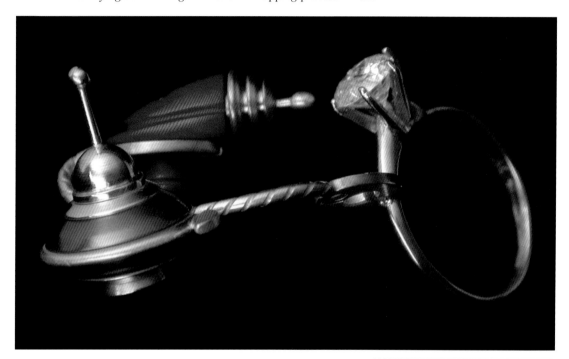

Mark Rooker

Entropus pseudoexorbitans debeeriae | 2006

3.5 X 4.5 X 2.5 CM

Recycled 10-karat yellow gold solitaire setting, laser-shot cubic zirconium, sterling silver, niobium, aluminum, yellow brass, 14-karat gold; fabricated, turned, carved, anodized

PHOTOS BY ARTIST

Kenneth C. MacBain
Wedding Rings | 2003

LEFT, 5.7 X 7.6 X 3.8 CM; RIGHT, 5.7 X 5.7 X 3.2 CM
Steel, cubic zirconia; machine cut, soldered

PHOTO BY ARTIST

Frédéric Braham
Untitled | 1993

2.4 X 2.4 X 0.6 CM
18-karat white gold;
soldered, sandblasted

PHOTO BY ARTIST

Jens Clausen

Hunn-Hann | 2006

LARGER, 2.6 X 2.6 X 1.2 CM;
SMALLER, 2.4 X 2.4 X 1.1 CM

Sterling silver, stainless steel;
mounted, turned, milled,
hand finished

PHOTOS BY ARTIST

Jan Wehrens

2 Wedding Rings | 2006

TALLER, 3.5 X 2.5 X 1.2 CM

18-karat gold, silver

PHOTOS BY ARTIST

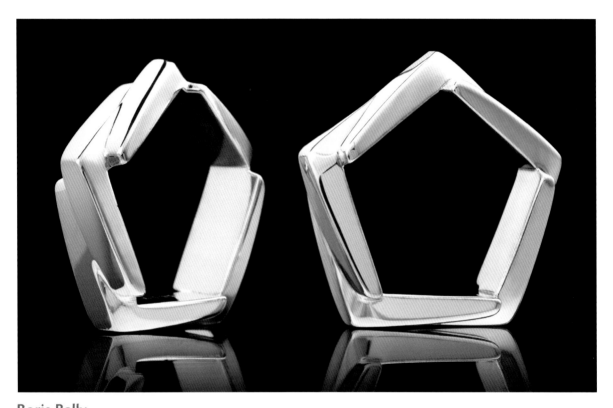

Boris Bally

Pentalap | 2007

3 X 3 X 1 CM
Recycled 18-karat white gold;
hand carved, lost wax cast

PHOTO BY J. W. JOHNSON PHOTOGRAPHY

Hirose Chibimaru Tomonori

Balance | 2007

LEFT, 2.2 X 2.2 X 0.6 CM;
RIGHT, 2.1 X 2.1 X 0.6 CM

Zirconium, tantarium, brown diamond,
white diamond, titanium, platinum

PHOTOS BY ARTIST

DIAMONDS CAN *be added at any time to symbolize the years, occasions, and events in one's marriage.* —ST

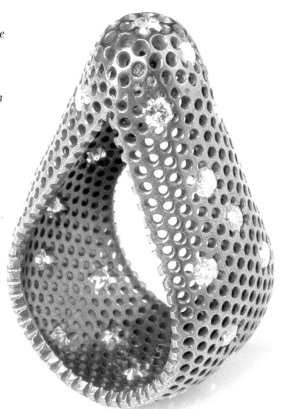

Salima Thakker

Grid Collection | 2006

3.8 X 1.5 CM
Rodium plated silver, diamonds; pierced

PHOTO BY ARTIST

Osamu Matsumoto

A Bolt from the Blue | 2006

2.2 X 2.2 X 0.6 CM
Platinum, titanium; machined,
pressed, set, oxidized

PHOTO BY ARTIST

Ryota Sakamoto

Iris | 2005

2.2 X 2.2 X 0.6 CM
Titanium, duralumin; expansive diffusion
bonded, machined, oxidized

PHOTO BY ARTIST

So Maruyama

Bearing | 2005

2.3 X 2.3 X 0.6 CM

Titanium, synthetic sapphire, synthetic ruby;
milled, lathe carved

PHOTO BY ARTIST

FIND YOUR *bearings.* —SM

A MINIMALIST *design celebrating the nontraditional couple.* —SK

Stephen Kris

RockStar | 2005

3 X 1.5 CM
18-karat grey gold, black diamond, rubies; fabricated

PHOTO BY RALPH GABRINER

Philippe Tournaire

Free Ring | 2006

2.5 X 1.2 X 0.1 CM
Platinum, diamond

PHOTO BY ARTIST

Phil Carrizzi

Engage | 2000

2.2 X 2.2 X 0.6 CM

Stainless steel; lathe turned,
milled, carved

PHOTOS BY DOUG YAPLE
COLLECTION OF STACIE CARRIZZI

ASKED TO *design an object for a wedding, I proposed to weave together the rituals associated with wedding rings and chalices. The result is a set of two "fitted" goblets, designed in a way that would naturally shape the wearers' hands into a cup. During a small ceremony staged in a private chapel, the bride and groom wore the goblets and then proceeded to drink from each other's hands, sharing wine from this ephemeral chalice, after putting on a ring.* —BL

Benjamin Lignel
Wedding Goblets | 1996

LEFT, 14 X 8.8 X 6 CM; RIGHT, 12 X 9 X 7 CM
Sterling silver; lost wax cast

PHOTO BY JOËL DEGEN

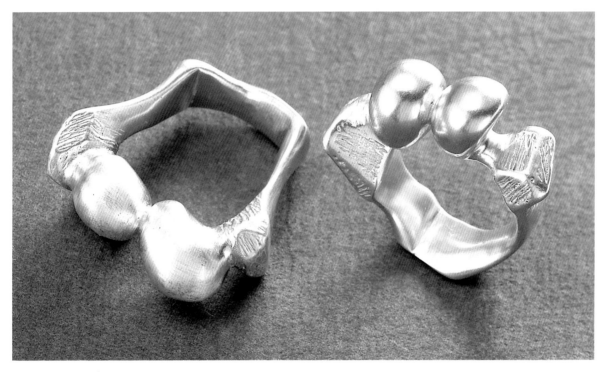

Hsia-Man Lydia Wang

Honey, I Love You | 2005–2006

3.5 X 3 X 1 CM
Sterling silver; cast

PHOTO BY ARTIST

Edward Lane McCartney

Wedding Bands | 2005

EACH, 0.5 X 2.5 X 2.5 CM

14-karat white gold; chased, fabricated,
hollow constructed

PHOTO BY JACK ZILKER

IN THE *serious commitment of marriage, sometimes you just need silliness.* —SV

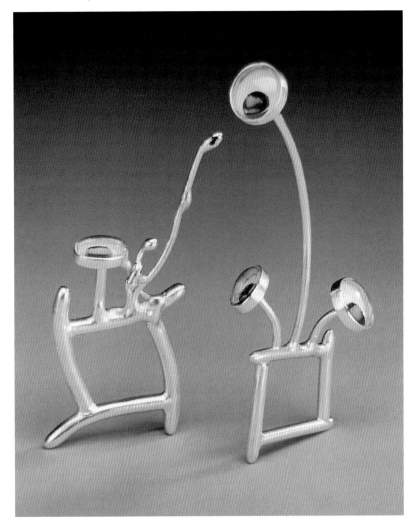

Shayla Vines

Well, Hello | 2006

LEFT, 6.4 X 3.8 X 0.8 CM;
RIGHT, 7.6 X 3.8 X 1.9 CM

Sterling silver, plastic
Googly eyes; fabricated

PHOTO BY DEAN POWELL

THIS SET *of twin rings is based on traditional Korean socks, called Beoseon. Wedding bands should make man and wife be one in body and spirit like socks should be one set.* —MK

Minwon Kim

A Set of Beoseon | 2006

LEFT, 2.5 X 2.4 X 1 CM;
RIGHT, 2.5 X 2.5 X 1 CM

Sterling silver, black pearls, white pearls; wax cast

PHOTOS BY BECKY MCDONAH

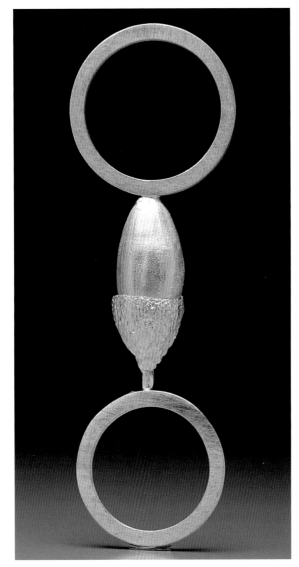

Yun Hee Kim

We Must Have Been a Couple | 2006

LEFT, 2.8 X 1.7 X 0.8 CM; RIGHT, 3.2 X 2 X 0.8 CM

Acorn, sterling silver; cast

PHOTOS BY MYUNG WOOK HUH, MUNCH STUDIO

Hui-Mei Pan

It's Hard to Pick | 2006

3.5 X 3.3 X 3.1 CM
Sterling silver, 18-karat yellow gold; fabricated

PHOTO BY ARTIST

Yuh-Shyuan Chen

Let's Get Married! | 2007

LEFT, 3.5 X 2 X 2 CM; RIGHT, 2.6 X 2.8 X 2 CM
Silver; fabricated

PHOTO BY ARTIST

THE MERGER *wedding band is about a marriage based more upon social and economic status than love.* —JB

Jim Bové
Merger | 2007

6.5 X 3.5 X 1.5 CM
Sterling silver, copper, patina; fabricated, cast

PHOTO BY ARTIST

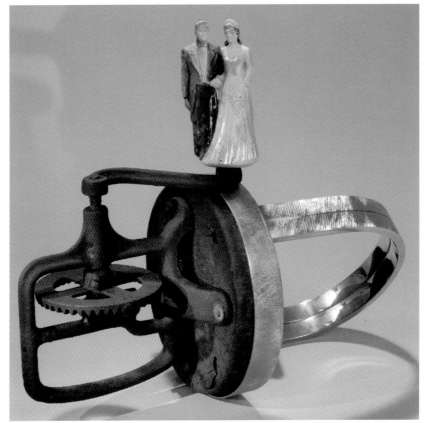

Jan Arthur Harrell

In Sickness and in Health
(Lady's Wedding Ring) | 2006

28 X 15 X 25 CM

Brass, 24-karat gold plate, plastic bride
and groom, rusted churn lid

PHOTOS BY JACK ZILKER

RINGS OF *betrothal often embody a specific idealized sentiment, an archetypal romantic ideal. Books, on the other hand, contain stories about how we live, the passage of time, and the changes we make. Turning an engagement or wedding ring into a book turns a singular and static ideal into an evolving story. The book/rings in* The Ring That Binds *series allow for fluctuations in meaning, honor passages, trace steps, and redefine the "fixed" idea of perfection as a process instead. They become symbols of a relationship that is ever-changing (for better and for worse) and is therefore more authentic. This "precious" collection of bound objects is an homage to the book as metaphor.* —ADK

Alyssa Dee Krauss

The Ring That Binds Series: The Book of Empty Promises, Volume II | 2002

3 X 2.2 X 0.4 CM
18-karat gold

PHOTO BY KEVIN DOWNEY

Jan Arthur Harrell

*Until Inertia Us Do Part
(Man's Wedding Ring)* | 2006

18 X 18 X 2 CM
Brass, gold plate, barbed wire

PHOTO BY JACK ZILKER

Kim Eric Lilot

Bi-Polar Ring | 2003

3.5 X 0.3 X 2.5 CM

18-karat gold, platinum, iridium; lost wax
cast, fabricated, chased

PHOTOS BY ARTIST

Christine Dwane

Cool Peace | 2005

2.3 X 1 X 2.3 CM
Titanium, fine silver, diamonds;
lathed, inlaid

PHOTO BY BAPTISTE GRISON

Ana Maria Dogoe Santos

Stone Ring | 2006

LEFT, 1.1 X 0.2 CM; RIGHT, 1.3 X 0.2 CM
Sterling silver

PHOTO BY JOSE DAVID PAZ RIVERO

Mark Herndon

Shotgun Wedding Rings | 2003

LEFT, 1.8 X 1.8 X 0.7 CM; RIGHT, 2.2 X 2.2 X 0.9 CM

Damascus steel, 18-karat palladium white gold,
22-karat yellow gold

PHOTO BY ARTIST
COLLECTION OF VERONICA DEANDA AND ERIK TOSTEN

Jill Newbrook

Untitled | 2004

1 X 2 CM
Silver, 18-karat gold; inlaid, photoetched

PHOTO BY JOËL DEGEN

G. Phil Poirier

Starry Night Bands | 2006

COMBINED, 2.5 X 2.5 X 2.5 CM

Stainless steel alloys, 18-karat gold;
mokume gane, forge welded

PHOTO BY ARTIST

Robin Cust

Untitled | 2006

2.5 X 2 X 0.5 CM

18-karat gold, found pitted steel; fabricated

PHOTO BY ROBERT DIAMANTE
COLLECTION OF JON WILSON AND SHERRY STREETER

ONE FOR *the day you met*

One for the day you fell in love

One for the day you married

These are great for alternative celebrations as well. —JJ

Just Jules

Celebration Bands | 2002

EACH, 0.3 CM WIDE
14-karat gold

PHOTO BY GEORGE POST

THE DIAMONDS *on this wedding ring are attached to the inner pink gold band only so that they can move from side to side as the outer band slides over the inner band.* —JB

Jane Bowden

Lisa's Ring | 2006

2.1 X 1.9 X 1.4 CM
18-karat pink gold, 18-karat
white gold, diamonds

PHOTO BY ARTIST

Keri Ataumbi

Square Bands, Circle Band, Stirrup Band, Square Plate Band | 2006

LEFT TO RIGHT: 2 X 2.5 X 0.3 CM, 2.5 X 2.5 X 0.3 CM, 2 X 2.5 X 0.3 CM, 3 X 2.5 X .3 CM

18-karat gold, diamonds; fabricated

PHOTOS BY ARTIST

Benjamin Lignel

Let's Splay | 2000

2.3 X 2.3 X 0.2 CM

18-karat gold; fabricated

PHOTO BY JOËL DEGEN

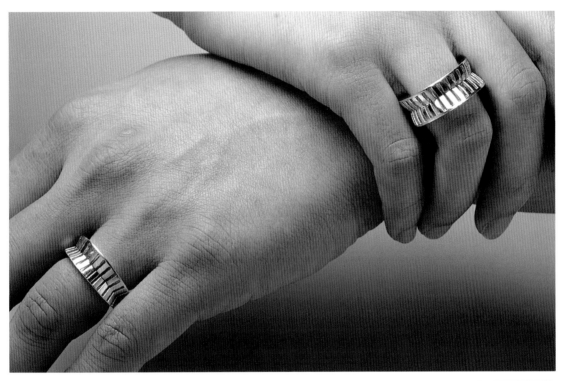

Yoon Joo-Young

The Infinite Ring | 2006

2.6 X 2.6 X 0.9 CM

14-karat gold; rapid prototyping, cast

PHOTOS BY MYUNG WOOK HUH, STUDIO MUNCH

Christa Lühtje
Untitled | 2002

2.3 X 1.3 CM
22-karat gold; forged, hand fabricated

PHOTO BY EVA JÜNGER

Jiro Kamata

Liebring | 2006

0.6 X 2.2 X 2.2 CM
18-karat gold

PHOTOS BY ARTIST

Matthew Crawford
Untitled | 2005

2.8 X 2.3 X 1 CM

14-karat white gold, 14-karat pink gold, pink sapphire, white diamond, natural pink diamond; fabricated, bead and bright cut set, prong set

PHOTO BY ARTIST

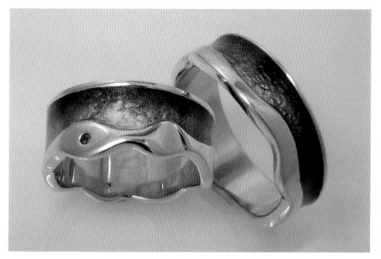

Cynthia Corio-Poli

Wedding Bell Blues | 2005

LEFT, 2 X 0.9 X 0.2 CM;
RIGHT, 2.2 X 0.7 X 0.2 CM

18-karat yellow gold, enamel,
rubies; wax carved, cast

PHOTO BY ARTIST

Philip Sajet

Two Is One | 1992

2.2 X 0.5 CM

18-karat gold, enamel

PHOTOS BY BEATE KLOCKMANN

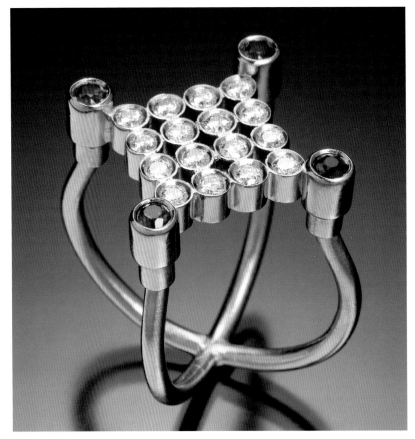

Michele Mercaldo

Sapphire Diamond Ring | 2005

2.5 X 2.1 X 2.1 CM

14-karat gold, diamonds, sapphires

PHOTOS BY ROBERT DIAMANTE
COURTESY OF MICHELE MERCALDO CONTEMPORARY JEWELRY DESIGN,
BOSTON, MASSACHUSETTS

Julie Mollenhauer
Untitled | 2005

0.4 X 2.2 X 2.2 CM
Gold, enamel

PHOTO BY THOMAS LENDEN

Claudio Pino
Enchanted Ring | 2006

3.5 X 2 X 1 CM
14-karat yellow gold, diamonds,
rubies, blue sapphires; constructed

PHOTO BY PHILOMÈNE LONGPRÉ

THIS RING *was created to remind its wearer of the archetype goddess within.* —SS

Sasha Samuels

Temple Ring | 2002

2.8 X 2.8 X 2.2 CM

18-karat lemon gold, platinum, context-cut
diamond, natural canary diamonds,
white Russian diamonds; cast

PHOTO BY DANIEL VAN ROSSEN

Eva Claire Martin

Diamond Morse Code Ring | 2006

2.4 X 2.1 X 0.5 CM

18-karat yellow gold, white, yellow,
cognac and chocolate diamonds

PHOTO BY ARTIST

John Leonard

Untitled | 2005

2.5 X 2.5 X 0.4 CM
18-karat gold; cast

PHOTO BY HAP SAKWA

Lezlie Jane

To Guinevere, from Arthur | 2005

2.2 X 2 X 1.6 CM
18-karat yellow gold, diamonds, rubies

PHOTO BY DOUG YAPLE

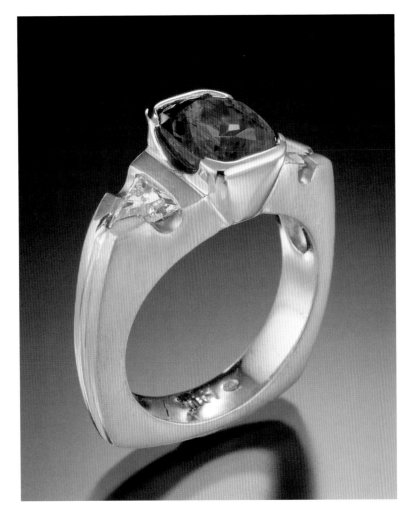

Linda M. Weiss

Tanzanite Ring | 2003

2.5 X 2.2 X 1 CM
Platinum, 18-karat gold, tanzanite, diamonds

PHOTO BY HAP SAKWA

Thomas Shamy

Jul Lea Ring | 2004

WIDTH, 0.4 CM

Platinum, 18-karat pink gold, diamond, garnets; hand carved, wax cast

PHOTO BY ARTIST

Jan Daggett

Elongated Marquis- and Princess-Cut Diamonds in 18-Karat White and Yellow Gold | 2004

2.5 X 2.1 X 1.2 CM

18-karat white gold, 18-karat yellow gold, diamonds; hard wax carved, lost wax cast

PHOTO BY ARTIST

Ingeborg Vandamme
Wedding-Ring III | 1995

2 X 1 X 3.5 CM
Silver, paper; soldered

PHOTOS BY HENNIE VAN BEEK
PRIVATE COLLECTION

THIS WEDDING ring is made of sterling silver and is shaped in the form of a house. It is engraved with Hebrew words from a traditional Jewish wedding song called "A Voice of Happiness, a Voice of Joy." This is a modern wedding ring inspired by ancient Jewish tradition, in which the design of the ring symbolizes the forming of a new Jewish household and family. —DBD

Dorit Bouskila Dehan
Kol Sason Vekol Simcha | 2001

3 X 2.2 X 0.7 CM
Sterling silver; hand fabricated

PHOTOS BY EITHAN SHUKER
COURTESY OF STUDIO TZERUFIM, D.N. MENASHE, ISRAEL

Nicole Jacquard

Lattice Wedding Ring | 2000

2.5 X 2.5 X 0.5 CM

18-karat white gold, diamonds; granulation,
hand fabricated, set

PHOTO BY KEVIN MONTAGUE

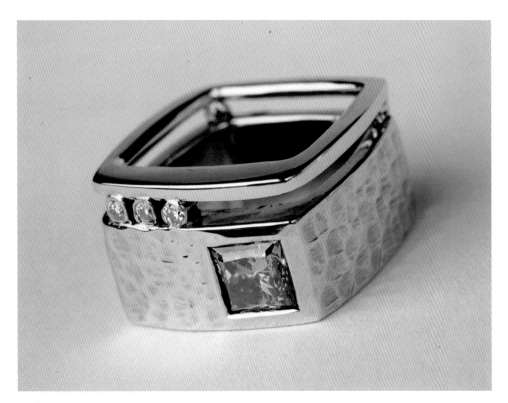

Hele

Wave | 2007

2.2 X 2.2 X 0.8 CM

Platinum, 14-karat yellow gold, white, blue,
and yellow diamonds; cast

PHOTO BY BLASER PHOTOGRAPHY
COURTESY OF GOLDSMITH SILVERSMITH, INC., OMAHA, NEBRASKA

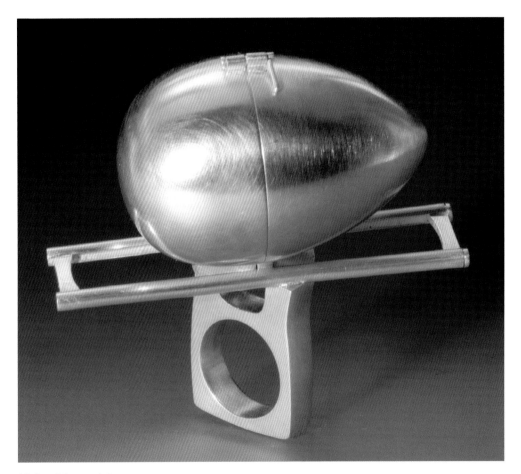

Yoko Noguchi

Untitled | 2006

6.5 X 6.5 X 3 CM

Sterling silver, 14-karat white gold, white
diamond, blue diamond; cast, fabricated

PHOTOS BY ARTIST

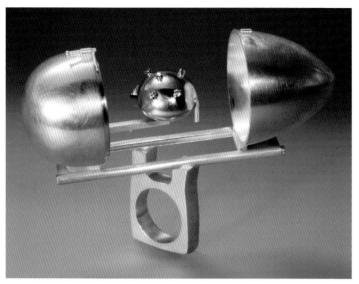

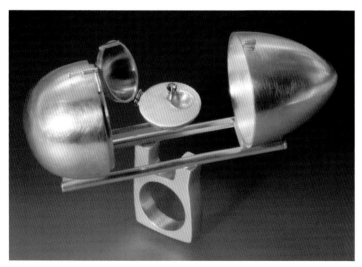

THE MULTIPLE *layers of this ring symbolize the different levels of feelings inside your heart. The outer egg shape represents your heart. The act of opening the egg shape is intended to invoke contemplation about opening one's heart. The diamonds on the dome shape reflect the sparkle of the heart from romance. As the dome shape is opened, you move deeper into the heart. There you find a hemispherical indentation whose rim forms a ring shape with a blue diamond on one side. The rim and diamond shape suggest a wedding ring. It is at the deepest level of the heart that you find true love represented by the inner-most ring. The blue diamond ring at the deepest part of the heart does not change.* —YN

Eun Mi Kim

I Trust You | 2005

0.8 X 1.7 X 2.5 CM

Sterling silver; soldered, kum boo,
hand fabricated, cold connected

PHOTOS BY ARTIST AND MYUNG WOOK HUH

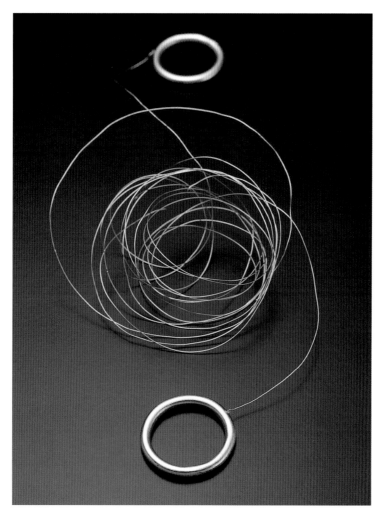

Yun Hee Kim

Untitled | 2006

2 X 2 X 0.3 CM
Sterling silver

PHOTO BY ARTIST

Shihoko Ogawa

Happiness | 2006

LARGER, 2.5 X 2.3 X 0.6 CM; SMALLER, 2 X 1.8 X 0.4 CM

Silver, brass, sapphire

PHOTOS BY SYOHEI

Haley Reneé Bates

A Modest Proposal | 2001

ENGAGEMENT RING: 0.9 X 0.1 X 0.8 CM
18-karat gold, diamond; formed, fabricated

PHOTOS BY ARTIST

THE LATIN inscriptions inside the rings read:

His: "Caelum Exultet," which translates, "Let Heaven Rejoice!"

Hers: "Terra Laetetur," which translates, "Let Earth Be Glad!" —AMLS

Anjanette M. Lemak Sidaway
Psalm 96: 11–12 | 1997

LARGER, 0.8 X 2.2 X 0.3 CM;
SMALLER, 0.6 X 2.2 X 0.3 CM

14-karat white gold, 14-karat yellow gold;
hand engraved, formed, soldered

PHOTO BY ARTIST

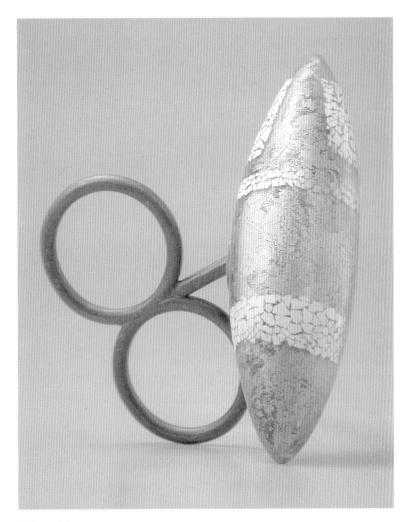

Jillian Moore

Double Eggs | 2005

6.5 X 4.5 X 5 CM

Sterling silver, resin,
gold leaf, eggshells

PHOTO BY TONY BOEHLER

PLAYING WITH *issues of display, these rings are a collection and symbol for the relationships that we have over time. Do all those relationships become similar when time deletes details?* —LBM

Lauren B. McAdams
15 Rings for 25 Boxes (Hackneyed) | 2006

38.1 X 57.2 X 69.9 CM

Jewelry boxes, silver, brass, imitation cubic zirconia; fabricated, riveted, set

PHOTO BY ARTIST

Visintin Graziano

Untitled | 2001

LEFT, 1.9 X 1.9 CM; RIGHT, 2 X 2 CM

Yellow gold, white gold

PHOTO BY FRANCO STORTI
COURTESY OF TINA ZAMBUSI

Maarten Van Der Vegte
*18-Karat Yellow Gold Bar
(Elements Series)* | 2006

7 X 4 X 2 CM
24-karat gold, silver, copper,
wood, messing

PHOTO BY SUSANNE QUAKKELAAR

Gésine Hackenberg

*Op Elk Potje Past Een Dekseltje
(Every Little Pot Has a Fitting Lid)* | 2005

TOP, 0.3 X 0.3 CM;
BOTTOM, 0.2 X 0.2 CM

Pure gold; welded, engraved

PHOTO BY ARTIST

Sergey Jivetin

Simple Synchronicity Bands | 2007

EACH, 2 X 0.4 X 2 CM

Jeweler's saw blades, silver

PHOTO BY ARTIST

THESE RINGS *were commissioned by a multimedia artist who mainly works on Internet projects. Her ring includes a white LED that lights up when his ring touches it. This can happen every time they hold hands. His ring is a bit smaller and more practical, having only the magnet, or "lighter," on it.* —JMK

Julia Maria Künnap
Light My Fire | 2004

LARGE, 2.5 X 2.5 X 0.7 CM;
SMALL, 2.2 X 2.2 X 0.3 CM

18-karat white gold, LED, battery,
herkon switch, magnet

PHOTOS BY ARTIST
PRIVATE COLLECTION

Maya Kini

Ceremonial Marking 1 | 2006

0.8 X 3 X 3 CM
Graphite; carved, machined

PHOTO BY KATIE MACDONALD

Stefan Heuser

Connect | 2006

2.4 X 0.4 CM
Lodestones, magnets

PHOTO BY ARTIST

I HAVE incorporated many identifiable symbols and images into my work and believe that creating tension through the juxtaposition of imagery, color, and meaning entices the viewer to seek an understanding that extends beyond the symbol itself. Although my work is very personal, it strikes a chord with people of many different backgrounds and lifestyles; there exists a common understanding of oppression, perseverance, and the search for identity. —ST

Sarah Troper
It's Just Plumbing: Parts M and F | 2005

LEFT, 2.8 X 2.8 X 2.2 CM; RIGHT, 2.5 X 2.5 X1.5 CM
Sterling silver, freshwater pearls; cast, fabricated, oxidized

PHOTOS BY SHONA KEARNEY

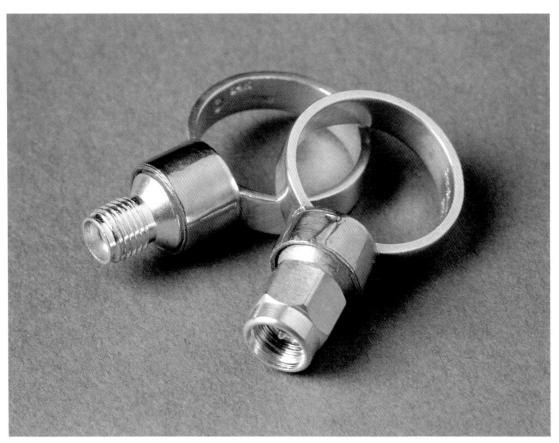

Jana Brevick

Screwing/Screwed | 2000

3.5 X 2.1 X 1.6 CM
24-karat gold, sterling silver; fabricated

PHOTOS BY ROGER SCHREIBER

EACH OF *the wives' rings reflects the manner in which the marriage ended. For example, if she was beheaded, the ring is cut in half. The king's ring has a running tally of the total number of wives.* —KBS

Kit Burke-Smith

Wedding Rings for King Henry VIII and His Wives | 1999

LEFT, 3 X 3 X 1. 5 CM; RIGHT, 2.5 X 2.5 X 0.5 CM
Silver, gold plate

PHOTO BY MARK JOHNSTON

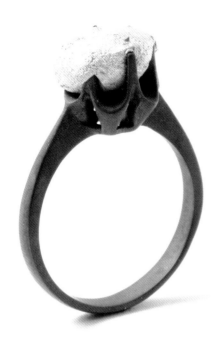

Karl Fritsch

Untitled | 2006

2.5 X 2.2 X 0.5 CM

White gold, gold; oxidized, cast

PHOTO BY ARTIST

Teresa Lane

Shotgun Wedding Ring II | 2006

2.4 X 2.4 X 2.8 CM

Mild steel, silver solder

PHOTO BY ARTIST

I WANTED *to make rings that were little love letters. Cloudy white plastic and layered black text create the largely hidden story of love.* I've Loved You since the Moment I Met You *and* I Want to Be Your Wife Always *are like wearing a dream or a memory of a thought. The woman's ring exudes love and the man's ring presents a stoic exterior, but each hold depths of private loving thoughts.* —CB

Colleen Baran

I've Loved You since the Moment I Met You and I Want to Be Your Wife Always | 2006

LEFT, 0.8 X 2.3 X 2.3 CM;
RIGHT, 1.2 X 2.1 X 2.1 CM

Plastic, thread, ink; hand fabricated

PHOTO BY ARTIST

Libelle/P.L.D'O

FOTO Memory of You | 2005

LEFT, 0.6 X 0.2 X 4.5 CM; RIGHT, 0.8 X 0.2 X 6.2 CM

Stein, gold, resin-foto; metal winched

PHOTO BY SASA CECILIA ESPINOZA

Jimin Park

Wedding Ring Series | 2006

EACH, 7 X 5 X 5 CM

Candle, paper, resin, plastic,
felt, sterling silver, diamonds

PHOTO BY MYUNG-WOOK HUH

LIKE TWINS, *independent forms arise from two double cylinders that are connected in the origin. Through the forging process, the rings are individualized in size and form. They are separated by the couple.* —NW

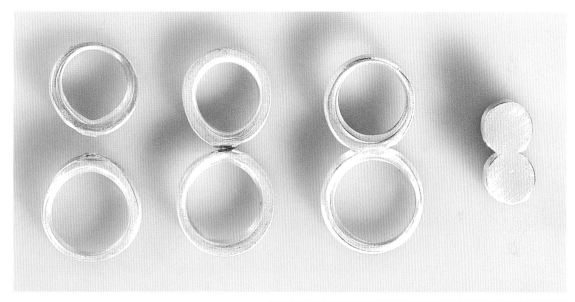

Nicole Walger

*Double Cylinder Rings—
The Individualized* | 2003

EACH, 1 X 2 X 1 CM
Fine gold, fine silver; punched, split, expanded

PHOTOS BY PETRA JASCHKE

Christine J. Brandt

Chica Dee | 2006

6.5 X 2.5 X 5 CM
Tagua nut, calcite crystals; hand carved, set

PHOTO BY MICHAEL BRANDT

THE BRIDE *and the groom each wear half a crown.* —TN

Ted Noten

Alternatives for Wedding Rings 2 | 1997

3 X 2.2 X 1 CM

18-karat gold, acrylic; cast, cut

PHOTO BY ARTIST
PRIVATE COLLECTION

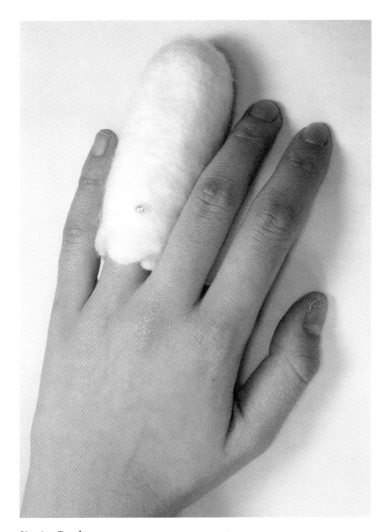

Jimin Park

Felt Wedding Ring I | 2006

9 X 3.5 X 3.5 CM

Felt, sterling silver, diamond

PHOTO BY ARTIST

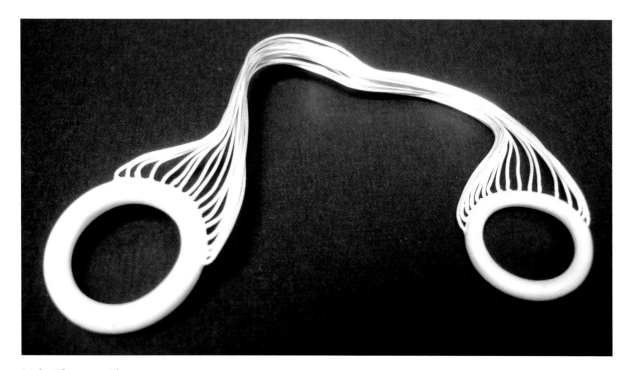

Yuh-Shyuan Chen

Forever Together | 2007

8 X 6 X 0.5 CM
Silver; fabricated

PHOTO BY ARTIST

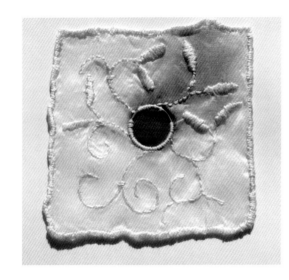

Kathryn Yeats
Untitled | 2007

8 X 8 CM
18-karat gold, silk, rust, thread; fabricated,
oxidized, hand embroidered

PHOTO BY ARTIST

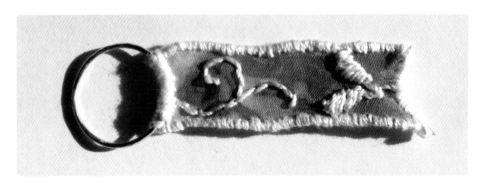

Kathryn Yeats
Untitled | 2007

2 X 6 CM
18-karat gold, silk, thread,
rust; fabricated, oxidized,
hand embroidered

PHOTO BY ARTIST

Jan Arthur Harrell

*In Sickness and in Health
(Lady's Engagement Ring)* | 2006

22 X 15 X 10 CM
Brass, 24-karat gold plate, rusted
air filter, glass, sterling silver

PHOTO BY JACK ZILKER

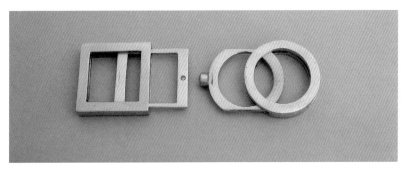

Yael Friedman

Couple | 2005

0.5 X 2.3 X 2.3 CM

Brass, copper, cubic zirconia;
hand fabricated

PHOTOS BY ARTIST

BY PLACING *the "engagement ring" between the two cups, the question arises: Does the relationship hold the communication together or tear it apart?* —LBM

Lauren B. McAdams

He Said, She Said… | 2005–2006

17.5 X 75 X 10 CM

Copper, silver, cubic zirconia; raised, fabricated, woven, hollow constructed

PHOTOS BY ARTIST

Stefano Marchetti
Untitled | 1998

2.1 X 2 X 1.8 CM
Gold; welded, etched

PHOTO BY ARTIST

Rickson Salkeld
Wedding Rings for Mom | 2006

1 X 2 X 2 CM
14-karat gold; lost wax cast

PHOTO BY ARTIST

Dahlia Kanner

Cork Rings | 1998

EACH, 0.5 X 1.2 X 0.2 CM
Sterling silver; cast

PHOTO BY MARK JOHNSON

THE IDEA *of marriage is complicated these days, not as naïve and romantic as it used to be. To express my mixed feelings on the issue, I chose images of children from a 1950s book. They are holding a red flower, as if they are asking, "Will you marry me?"* —MBOS

Michal Bar-On Shaish
Untitled | 2006

9 X 3 CM
Fine iron binding wire; filigree

PHOTO BY LEONID PADRUL

Julie Mollenhauer

Les Jeux sont faits/Faites vos jeux | 2005

0.8 X 2.5 X 2.5 CM
14-karat gold

PHOTO BY THOMAS LENDEN

Asato Phillip Tanaka

The True Wedding Ring II | 2006

2 X 2 X 3 CM
Silver, 18-karat gold, commercial
figurine; soldered, cast

PHOTO BY ARTIST

David A. Casella

Woven Chain Rings | 2006

LEFT, 2.5 X 1 X 0.4 CM; RIGHT, 2 X 1 X 0.4 CM

Fine silver, 22-karat yellow gold;
fused, hand woven

PHOTO BY ARTIST

CONTEMPORARY MARRIAGES *often include children as well as the two partners. The four stones represent the people in the marriage. The fitting of the three sections shows the interconnectedness of the whole group.* —KM

Katharina Möller
The Perfect Fit | 1995

TOGETHER, 2.5 X 2.5 X 1.9 CM
18-karat yellow gold, 18-karat nickel
white gold, diamonds; cast, fabricated

PHOTOS BY ARTIST

Barbara Stutman

Queen for a Day | 1995

5.9 X 4.7 X 2.4 CM

18-karat gold, fine silver, sterling silver commercial wedding band; spool knitted, knitted, cast

PHOTO BY PIERRE FAUTEUX

Ruslana Zitserman

Tangled Connections, Psyche | 2006

1.2 X 2.5 X 2.5 CM

Sterling silver, copper; chain mail

PHOTO BY ARTIST

Pavé Fine Jewelry
Untitled | 2006

3 X 1.4 X 0.9 CM

14-karat white gold, 14-karat yellow gold, natural
green sapphire, white diamonds; lost wax cast

PHOTO BY ARTIST

Sora Maruyama

Chew-ring | 2004

2.3 X 2.3 X 0.5 CM
Pure platinum, pure gold; chewed

PHOTO BY ARTIST

NO TOOLS *except teeth.* —SM

Erik Urbschat

Pure Metal Rings | 2006

AVERAGE, 2 X 2 X 1.2 CM

Silver, gold, platinum, palladium; forged

PHOTOS BY ARTIST

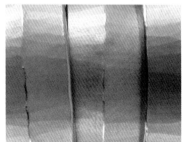

THE SQUARE *becomes a circle and the circle a square;*
he and she are mixed and form one entity. —YF

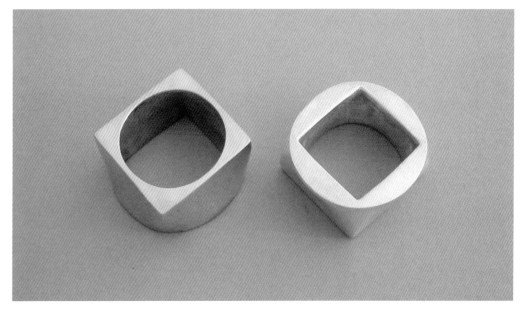

Yael Friedman
Rounding the Edges | 2003

1.2 X 2.5 X 2.5 CM
Sterling silver, brass; hand fabricated

PHOTO BY ARTIST

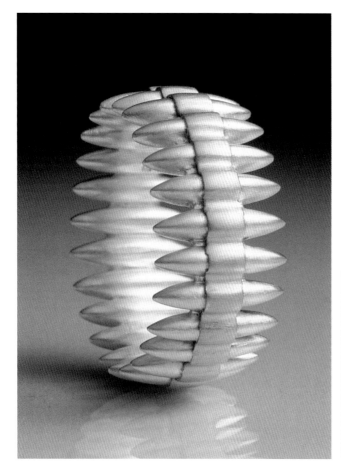

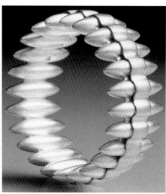

Mark Nuell

Untitled | 2004

2.5 X 1.2 X 2.5 CM

Silver, 22-karat gold; cast, fabricated

PHOTOS BY FXP PHOTOGRAPHY

Pamela Froman

Jay's Crush | 2006

2.6 X 2.6 X 1 CM

18-karat yellow gold, platinum; crushed finish

PHOTO BY JAY LAWRENCE GOLDMAN

So Maruyama

Dots | 2004

2.2 X 2.2 X 0.7 CM
Titanium, platinum, orange gold; inlaid

PHOTO BY ARTIST

Joan Tenenbaum

Tundra Patterns Wedding Rings | 2001

0.7 X 2.2 X 2.2 CM

14-karat gold, 22-karat gold, sterling silver;
hand fabricated, mokume gane, etched

PHOTO BY DOUG YAPLE

James E. Binnion

Mokume Wedding Ring | 2005

0.7 X 0.2 CM
18-karat yellow gold, 14-karat palladium white gold,
14-karat red gold, platinum; mokume gane

PHOTO BY HAP SAKWA

Eva Bragsjö
Untitled | 2006

1 X 2.5 X 2.5 CM
Silver

PHOTO BY PETTER MÖRK

Atsuko Honma

Hug | 2003

2.3 X 2.3 X 0.8 CM
Platinum, pink gold; welded, stamped

PHOTOS BY ARTIST

THIS RING *is a visual metaphor for the way that two people entwine their lives into one future together. At the same time, it is a pun on the phrase "tie the knot."* —CE

Cynthia Eid

Knot | 1985

2.5 X 2.2 X 0.5 CM

14-karat yellow gold;
wax worked, cast

PHOTO BY ARTIST

Maureen Padgett

Baskets | 2005

LARGEST, 1.2 X 2.5 X 2.5 CM
18-karat yellow gold; cast

PHOTO BY ARTIST

1311
Joe Korth

Sparks Rings | 2006

EACH, 2 X 2 X 0.5 CM
Copper, silver; fabricated

PHOTO BY ARTIST
COURTESY OF CLEAR CREEK ACADEMY OF JEWELRY
AND METAL ARTS, DENVER, COLORADO

Sora Maruyama

Guardian Dragon | 2006

2.2 X 2.2 X 0.8 CM

Platinum, pink gold, diamond;
engraved, high pressure transfer

PHOTO BY ARTIST

Katsue Imoue

Mokume Gane | 2006

2.3 X 2.3 X 0.8 CM
Platinum, white gold;
mokume gane, stamped

PHOTO BY ARTIST

Dwaine Ferguson

Untitled | 2006

2.2 X 2.2 X 1.4 CM

14-karat yellow gold, baguette diamond; cast

PHOTO BY BLASER PHOTOGRAPHY
COURTESY OF GOLDSMITH SILVERSMITH, INC., OMAHA, NEBRASKA

Andy Cooperman

Lashed Bands | 2000

0.6 X 0.2 CM

14-karat white gold, 14-karat rose gold,
18-karat yellow gold; fabricated

PHOTO BY DOUG YAPLE

THREE RED *gold rings are fixed in place. The white gold ring is free and can turn around.* —MZ

Michael Zanin
Ring 3x3+0 (Engagement Ring) | 2006

2.5 X 2.7 X 1.2 CM
18-karat red gold, white gold, diamonds

PHOTOS BY ARTIST

Josephine Bergsøe

Care | 2006

0.3 X 2.5 CM

18-karat white gold, 22-karat red gold, ruby; hand fabricated, soldered

PHOTO BY SARA LINDBAEK

Sicuro Giovanni Minto

Federica and Davide | 2006

EACH, 2 X 2 CM

18-karat gold; fabricated

PHOTO BY ARTIST
PRIVATE COLLECTION

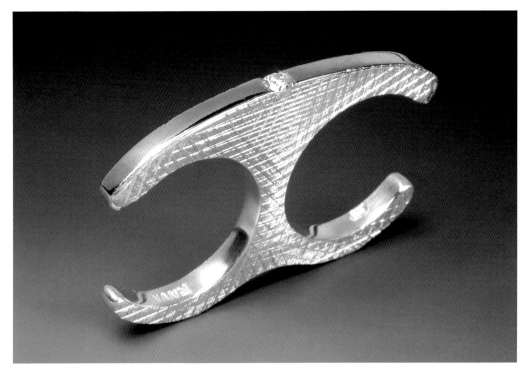

Nanz Aalund

Two-Finger Wedding Band | 2005

2.7 X 4.1 X 0.3 CM

Platinum, sterling silver, 24-karat gold, diamond; cast, fabricated

PHOTO BY JIM FORBES

THIS RING *is to be worn between the second and third fingers of the left hand. It identifies the duality of life and suggests a bridge between the two fingers: bridges of communication and balance that will allow the relationship to thrive. Brass knuckles are also suggested by this ring, with the intention to remind each partner that they may have to fight societal conventions, complacency, and temptation to maintain the marriage they want.* —NA

THIS TENSION *setting brings maximum light and refraction to a large diamond or gemstone.* —JK

John Kuhta

Everyone Will Know You're Engaged to Me | 2007

3 X 2 X 1.5 CM

Sterling silver, 18-karat gold, cut crystal; fabricated, tension set

PHOTO BY ARTIST

WE'VE BEEN *together for 40 years and last year for our anniversary, we made this wedding ring together. I hadn't worn a wedding ring for more than 30 years because I was always working with my hands. We always remembered anyway.* —RW & DW

Roberta Williamson and David Williamson

Remember How Much I Love You | 2005

2 X 3.5 X 2 CM

18-karat gold; carved, lost wax cast, fabricated, soldered, sandblasted, polished, engraved

PHOTO BY RALPH GABRINER

Joseé Desjardins

Bonds | 2006

AVERAGE, 3 X 3.5 X 1.5 CM

Sterling silver, 18-karat gold; hand fabricated

PHOTO BY ANTHONY MCLEAN
COURTESY OF GALERIE NOËL GUYOMARC'H, MONTREAL, QUEBEC, CANADA

Jessica Fields

Diamond Clover Band | 2004

0.5 X 2.1 X 0.3CM
18-karat yellow gold, diamonds; cast

PHOTO BY JOHN CURRY

Wesley Glebe

Slavi's Ring | 2006

1 X 2 X 0.2 CM
Titanium, 24-karat gold, diamonds,
14-karat white gold

PHOTO BY ARTIST

Kathleen Diresta-Roth

Wedding Ring Series | 2004

4.5 X 1.5 CM
14-karat gold, 18-karat gold,
diamond, platinum

PHOTO BY CHRISTOPHER WEIL

Jan Daggett

*Natural Orange-Gold Diamond in
18-Karat White and Yellow Gold,
2-Ring Set* | 2004

EACH, 2.4 X 2.1 X 1.1 CM
18-karat white gold, 18-karat yellow gold,
orange-gold diamond; hard wax carved,
lost wax cast

PHOTO BY ARTIST

Garry VannAusdle

Wheat Design Wedding Bands | 2006

EACH, 0.7 X 0.7 CM

14-karat yellow gold, diamond; hard wax carved,
lost wax cast, recarved, set

PHOTO BY ARTIST

Cesar Lim and Vlad Lavrovsky

Wedding Band | 2006

2 X 2 X 2 CM
18-karat gold, diamonds; hand fabricated,
channel set, bezel set

PHOTO BY ARTIST

THE PROFILE *of this ring sits low for everyday wear.* —SS

Sasha Samuels

Wide Wing Band | 2003

2.1 X 2.1 X 1.1 CM

18-karat white gold, 18-karat lemon gold,
canary diamonds; cast, hand fabricated,
bezel set

PHOTO BY DANIEL VAN ROSSEN
COLLECTION OF LAINIE COLBURN

Josephine Bergsøe

Untitled | 2003

2 X 2 X 3.1 CM

22-karat gold, 24-karat gold,
silver, ruby, Tahitian pearl, diamonds;
hand fabricated, soldered, oxidized

PHOTO BY SARA LINDBAEK

Liaung Chung Yen

Untitled | 2006

LEFT, 2.5 X 2 X 0.5 CM; RIGHT, 2.5 X 2 X 0.2 CM

18-karat gold, rough diamond crystal,
rose-cut diamond; fabricated

PHOTO BY ARTIST

Daphne Milne Groos

Untitled | 2004

0.7 X 0.7 CM

18-karat yellow gold, black diamonds

PHOTO BY JAMES DEE

HE WEARS *her fingerprint, she wears his.* —GR

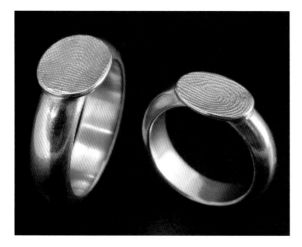

Gerd Rothmann

Stefan and Laura's Wedding Rings | 2002

LARGEST, 1 X 2.2 X 2.1 CM
18-karat gold; cast, fabricated

PHOTO BY STEFAN FRIEDEMANN
COURTESY OF ORNAMENTUM GALLERY, HUDSON, NEW YORK

Stefano Marchetti
Untitled | 1998

2.1 X 2 X 1.8 CM
Gold; welded, etched

PHOTO BY ARTIST

THE SAW *piercing is to get depth in the design. The chasing is to shape and texture the leaves, and the engraving is to trim and shade the flowers.* —TH

Thomas Herman

Leaf over Leaf and Flower and Leaf | 2006

EACH, 2.1 X 2.1 X 0.6 CM

18-karat yellow gold, diamonds; chased, saw pierced, engraved

PHOTO BY ALLEN BRYAN

Fritz J. Casuse

Cala | 2005

6 X 3.3 X 2.1 CM

18-karat gold, 14-karat white gold, pink cultured pearl, Mediterranean red coral, diamonds; hand carved, cast, fabricated

PHOTO BY PHIL KARSHIS

THIS PAIR *of rings can be worn individually, shared by two people, or stacked as a pair on one finger. To me, the dome evokes images of breasts and beehives, which can be seen as metaphors for fertility, nourishment, the hard work of individuals toward a common goal, and the simple beauty that is present when loving unconditionally.* —BS

Boline Strand

Milk & Honey | 2005

EACH, 2.5 X 1.9 X 1.2 CM
18-karat yellow gold, 22-karat
yellow gold, white diamonds;
hand fabricated, raised, bezel set

PHOTO BY TOM MILLS

Mariel Pagliai

My Diva Forever | 2005

2.2 X 2 X 2.2 CM
18-karat gold, diamonds

PHOTO BY ARTIST
PRIVATE COLLECTION

Bernhard Schobinger
Until Death Do Us Part | 2005

EACH, 2.5 X 2.5 X 1.8 CM

18-karat gold, diamonds, enamel

PHOTOS BY ARTIST

Karl Fritsch

Untitled | 2006

2.8 X 2.5 X 1.5 CM
Gold, diamonds, rubies, emeralds; cast

PHOTO BY ARTIST

Hratch Babikian

*Urchin Rings His
and Hers* | 2006

2.5 X 2.5 CM
14-karat gold;
cast, fabricated

PHOTO BY ARTIST

Kim-Jung Vu
My choice... | 2006

AVERAGE, 2.5 X 7 X 0.5 CM
Rubber, silver, acrylic paint

PHOTO BY ARTIST

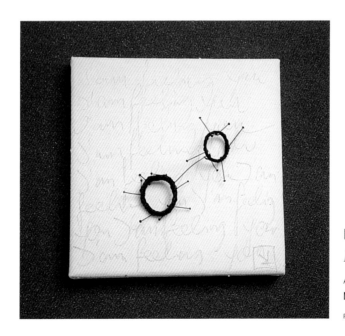

Kim-Jung Vu
I Am Feeling You... | 2006

AVERAGE, 3.5 X 7 X 2 CM
Nylon, acrylic paint

PHOTO BY ARTIST

Chi Yu-Fang

Rings | 2006

5 X 5 X 30 CM
Wire, nylon thread, cotton thread; wound

PHOTOS BY CHUANG-SHENG TSAI

Philipp Spillmann

Reindearrings | 2006

LARGE, 8 X 7 X 5 CM; SMALL, 5.5 X 5 X 3.5 CM

Sterling silver; constructed, oxidized, screwed

PHOTO BY ARTIST

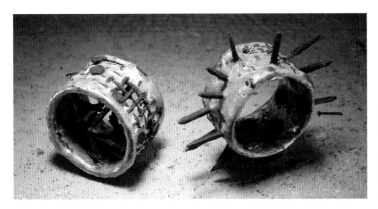

Federico Vianello

Wearable/Unwearable | 2005

EACH, 3.5 X 2 X 3.5 CM
Pure silver, iron nails, iron net

PHOTO BY DUILIO RINGRESSI

Hans Stofer

*Wedding Ring Set - One for
Each Day of the Week* | 2005

AVERAGE, 3 X 3 CM
Gold, silver, steel, pewter,
lead, copper, paint, coal

PHOTO BY ARTIST
COLLECTION OF ESTHER BRINKMANN

Karen J. Lauseng

Yield to Equality | 2001

6.4 X 2.5 X 0.3 CM
Sterling silver, thermoplastic

PHOTO BY ARTIST

Fritz Maierhofer

Wedding Rings for Aloha and Anatol | 2006

EACH, 0.1 X 0.2 CM
Acrylic, platinum

PHOTO BY ARTIST

THIS IS *a chat-up ring with a phone number in mirror writing. You can stamp it and leave your number behind.* —LB

Liesbet Bussche
I Just Called to Say I Love You | 2006

2 X 3.5 X 1 CM
Silver; sawed, soldered

PHOTOS BY ARTIST

Pam Ritchie

Untitled | 2006

ENGAGEMENT RING, 3.3 X 2.1 X 1.7 CM;
BAND, 0.7 X 1.9 X 1.9 CM

Sterling silver, rubber; CAD/CAM,
fabricated, cast

PHOTO BY ARTIST

Cláudia Cucchi
Untitled | 2003

5 X 4 X 3.5 CM
Silver, acrylic, photo

PHOTO BY FEDERICO CAVICCHIOLI

Elisa Gulminelli
*One-Day Commitment
Wedding Ring* | 2006

2.5 X 2.5 X 0.3 CM
Paper; cut

PHOTO BY ARTIST

THE JOKE *was too good to refuse!* —JB

Jana Brevick

Cat. 5 Compliant: Jacked | 2001

4.2 X 2 X 0.9 CM
Ethernet plug, socket, sterling silver; fabricated

PHOTOS BY ROGER SCHREIBER

Eric E. Okon

Engagement Set | 2002

4.5 X 2.5 X 2.5 CM

Plastic, white gold, diamond, steel,
silver, rose petals; cast, fabricated

PHOTOS BY ARTIST

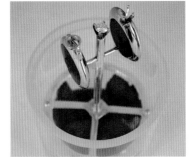

Chieko Arai
Blue Threads | 2006

EACH, 5.5 X 2.8 X 1 CM
Paper, silver, gold leaf; fabricated

PHOTO BY ARTIST

Chieko Arai

Red Threads | 2006

EACH, 4 X 3 X 1.3 CM
Paper, silver; fabricated

PHOTO BY ARTIST

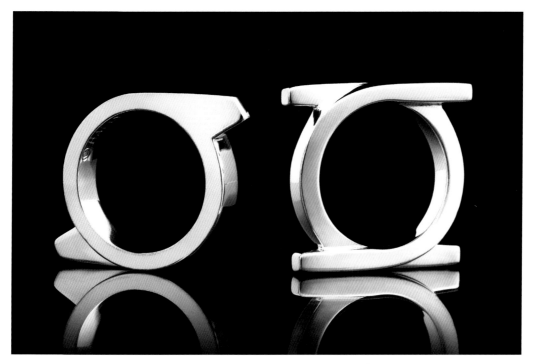

Boris Bally

Brace: Embrace | 2007

3 X 2.5 X 0.7 CM
Recycled 18-karat white gold;
hand carved, lost wax cast

PHOTOS BY J. W. JOHNSON PHOTOGRAPHY

Christine Dhein

Wedding Ring for Araya Diaz | 2000

3 X 2.5 X 1 CM

Platinum, sapphire; wax carved,
cast, finished, channel set

PHOTO BY ARTIST

Doug Bucci

Untitled | 2005

2.3 X 2.1 X 0.6 CM

14-karat gold, white sapphire; cast from
rapid prototyped solidscape protobuild

PHOTO BY PETER GROESBECK
COURTESY OF THE WEXLER GALLERY, PHILADELPHIA, PENNSYLVANIA

Sayuri Goto

White Clouds in the Blue Sky | 2006

2.5 X 2.5 X 0.8 CM

Zirconium; machined, engraved, oxidized

PHOTO BY ARTIST

Julia Behrends

Lock Love Engagement Ring | 2005

2.8 X 2.2 X 1.3 CM

Morganite, platinum, round diamonds;
CAD/CAM, bezel set

PHOTOS BY ROBERT DIAMANTE

TRIO REPRESENTS *a classical design with a modern interpretation. The simplicity of the three diamonds tension set allows appreciation of the whole stone in all its beauty.* —AN

Adam Neeley

Trio | 2006

2.8 X 2.3 X 0.5 CM

14-karat white gold, diamonds;
hand fabricated

PHOTO BY HAP SAKWA

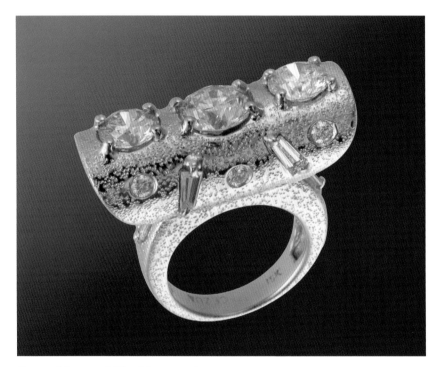

Cesar Lim and Vlad Lavrovsky

Marybetcha Engagement Ring | 2006

3 X 3.5 X 1.5 CM

18-karat gold, diamonds; lost wax cast,
fabricated, textured, flush set, prong set

PHOTO BY ARTIST
COLLECTION OF ELIZABETH ROXAS-DOBRISH

Jennifer Kellogg

Untitled | 2003

2.1 X 2.1 X 1 CM
18-karat white gold,
diamonds; pavé set

PHOTO BY LUIS ERNESTO SANTANA

Jean-Marc Garel

Tableau Ring | 2006

Quartz, diamonds, platinum

PHOTO BY DOMINO

Lisa Krikawa

Mokume Borealis | 2006

2.8 X 2 X 0.8 CM

Platinum, 14-karat white gold, sterling silver,
diamonds; CAD/CAM designed, mokume gane,
fabricated, repoussé, bezel set, pavé set

PHOTO BY HAP SAKWA

Lazare Kaplan International, Inc.

Lazare Virtue Square-Emerald-Cut Eternity Band | 2005

Platinum, diamonds; prong set

PHOTOS BY DARREN ROSARIO

Linda Weiss

Platinum Marquise Ring | 2005

2.5 X 2.3 X 1.3 CM

Platinum, diamonds; cast, engraved,
channel set, bezel set

ENGRAVING BY KEVORK HAGOPIAN
PHOTO BY HAP SAKWA
COLLECTION OF MRS. M. ULRICH

Eun-Jung Kim

Love of All | 2005

2.5 X 2.2 X 0.6 CM

18-karat gold, diamonds; cast, pavé set

PHOTOS BY MYUNG WOOK HUH, STUDIO MUNCH

Lisa Krikawa

Queen of Everything | 2006

2.6 X 2.1 X 1.1 CM

Platinum, 14-karat white gold, sterling silver, 10-karat green gold, light yellow-green, white, and black diamonds; CAD/CAM designed, mokume gane, fabricated, repoussé, channel set, bezel set, bead set, laser welded

PHOTO BY HAP SAKWA

Caleb Meyer

Ten Stone Platinum Ring | 2006

2.4 X 0.7 X 0.4 CM

Platinum, blue sapphires, round brilliant
diamonds; lost wax cast, bezel set

PHOTO BY ROBERT DIAMANTE

Eva Martin

Carousel Ring | 2006

2.1 X 2.1 X 0.6 CM

18-karat palladium white gold,
diamonds

PHOTO BY ARTIST

I WANTED *the gold to curve around the finger and blossom open to the beautiful gemstone, like a graceful flower.* —AN

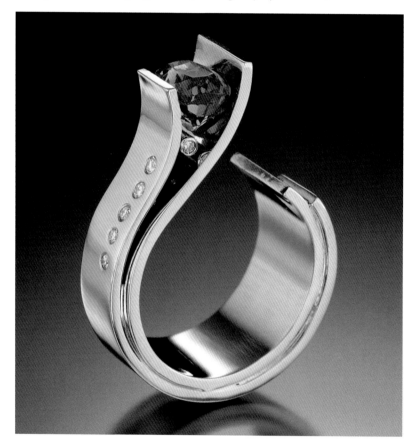

Adam Neeley

Fiore | 2006

3 X 2.3 X 0.8 CM
14-karat white gold, purple sapphire, diamonds; hand fabricated

PHOTO BY ARTIST

Sako Khatcherian

Untitled | 2006

2.5 X 1.5 X 1.5 CM

19-karat white gold,
blue diamonds; pavé set

PHOTO BY TANYA CLARK
COURTESY OF OBJECT DESIGN GALLERY,
VANCOUVER, BRITISH COLUMBIA, CANADA

Hsueh-Ying Wu

Wedding Gauze | 2006

AVERAGE, 3.1 X 2.8 X 1 CM
Sterling silver, copper, stainless steel mesh,
brass mesh; hand fabricated

PHOTO BY CHIN-TING CHIU

MARRIAGE TAKES *a lot of love and work. You start off with a rough diamond, and with a lot of love and hard work, you end with a brilliant one.* —CM

Claire Moens

Diamond in the Rough | 2005

LEFT, 1 X 2.5 CM; RIGHT, 0.5 X 2.1 CM

18-karat white gold, rough diamonds

PHOTO BY LUC VAN MUYLEM
PRIVATE COLLECTION

Jason Morrissey
Mokume Gane Bands | 2006

BOTTOM, 2 X 2 CM; TOP, 1.7 X 1.7 CM
Silver, nickel silver; mokume gane,
double laminated, twisted

PHOTO BY ROBERT DIAMANTE

THE DESIGN *is loosely based on the initials of the couple. The rings are cut from the same piece of metal and then exchanged. They are soldered onto a silver liner with a 9-karat gold line added to lady's ring.* —CL

Carole Leonard

Exchanged Metal Wedding Rings | 2006

EACH, 0.8 X 2.5 X 2.5 CM
Unhallmarked 18-karat white gold, silver,
9-karat red gold

PHOTO BY ARTIST
COLLECTION OF KATRINA WELLS AND MATT KIEFFER

Katharina Möller

Untitled | 1992

2.5 X 2.3 X 1.2 CM
18-karat yellow gold, 18-karat palladium white
gold, 18-karat nickel white gold, marble; inlaid

PHOTO BY ARTIST

Sawako Hirayama

Wave | 2006

2.2 X 2.2 X 0.7 CM

Platinum, white gold, pink gold;
mokume gane

PHOTO BY ARTIST

Suzanne Amendolara

Untitled II | 2006

2 X 2 CM
14-karat gold, diamond; cast

PHOTO BY ARTIST
COLLECTION OF KAREN ERNST AND ERIC CALDWELL

Barbara Paganin

Radiolare | 1992

3 X 3 X 1.5 CM
18-karat gold, silver; niello

PHOTO BY ARTIST

Caleb Meyer
Riveted Wedding Band Set | 2006

LARGER, 2.5 X 0.8 X 0.3 CM

18-karat yellow gold, platinum, round brilliant diamonds; hand forged, fabricated, bezel set

PHOTO BY ROBERT DIAMANTE

Paul Leathers
Wedding Set | 2006

2 X 2 X 0.8 CM

14-karat yellow gold, white gold, yellow diamond; depletion gilt, cast, bezel set

PHOTO BY ARTIST
PRIVATE COLLECTION

Birna Sigurbjornsdottir

The Warrior and the Elven King | 2005

LEFT, 1.2 X 0.8 X 0.4 CM;
RIGHT, 0.8 X 0.7 X 0.5 CM

Sterling silver, rutilated
quartz; cast

PHOTO BY HANK DREW
COLLECTION OF BRAN AND IAN LAFAE

THIS RING *is based on the Olomuc Synagogue in the Czech Republic and was made in the Jewish tradition. It was created as a tribute to the commissioner's father, who attended the synagogue.* —VAS

Vicki Ambery-Smith

Olomuc Synagogue | 2004

3.8 X 2.4 X 2.3 CM
Silver, rose gold; scored, folded

PHOTO BY ARTIST
PRIVATE COLLECTION

Naoko Matsumoto

Knot | 2005

2.2 X 3.8 X 1.2 CM

Tantalum, pink gold;
machined, hand carved

PHOTO BY ARTIST

Naoko Matsumoto

Impulse | 2006

LEFT, 2 X 2 X 0.7 CM;
RIGHT, 2.2 X 2.2 X 0.8 CM

Pink gold, titanium, tantalum;
machined, hammered

PHOTO BY ARTIST

Suzanne Amendolara

Untitled I | 2003

2.3 X 1.8 X 1.8 CM
Sterling silver, 14-karat white gold,
14-karat gold, diamond; mokume gane,
formed, fabricated, bezel set

PHOTO BY ARTIST
COLLECTION OF MR. AND MRS. JOHN MATHIE

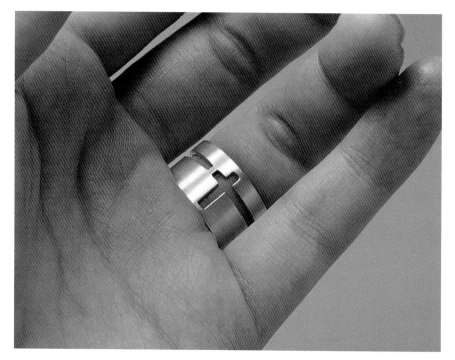

Jeemin Chung

Cherish | 2004

1 X 1.7 X 1.6 CM

Sterling silver; hand fabricated

PHOTOS BY MYUNG WOOK HUH, STUDIO MUNCH

Jessica Bojczuk

Commit | 2004

1 X 2 X 2 CM
Sterling silver, 9-karat gold;
hand fabricated

PHOTO BY JEREMY DILLION

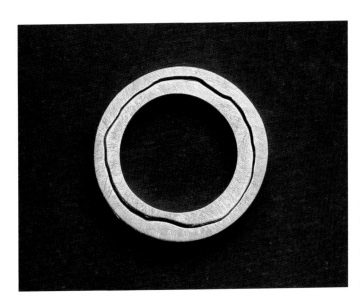

Andrzej Bielak

Untitled | 2006

2.4 X 0.4 CM
14-karat yellow gold; cut

PHOTO BY BARBARA KARISKA-BIELAK

Satoshi Sorayama

Connect | 2004

2.4 X 3.5 X 0.7 CM
Platinum, diamond; machined, screwed

PHOTOS BY ARTIST

Shelby Ferris Fitzpatrick

Double Rings | 2005

EACH, 5 X 4.4 X 4.4 CM

Silver, gold; inlaid

PHOTO BY MIKE BLISSETT
PRIVATE COLLECTION

Kiley Granberg

Untitled | 2006

2.5 X 2 X 1 CM
Brass, 24-karat gold plating

PHOTO BY CHARLES LEWTON-BRAIN

THE TWO *parts of the gear interact and work together to generate movement and energy. This is a metaphor for marriage.* —YCC

Yu-Chun Chen

Interact | 2002

BOTTOM, 3 X 3 X 0.7 CM;
TOP, 2.5 X 2.5 X 0.6 CM

Sterling silver

PHOTO BY ARTIST

Louise Tasker

Connect | 2005

2.4 X 2.4 X 0.9 CM
White gold, powdered steel,
resin; cast

PHOTO BY ARTIS

Daphne van der Meulen

Paper Ring | 2006

1 X 2 X 2 CM
Sterling silver; cast

PHOTO BY ARTIST

Rachael Fullerton

Wrapped Around | 2006

3.5 X 3.5 X 1 CM

Rubber, silver

PHOTO BY ARTIST

Sabina Lee

Love Tree | 2005

2.4 X 2.1 X 0.9 CM
18-karat black and white gold,
black and white diamonds; set

PHOTO BY LEO NG

LOVE TREE *is inspired by a classical Chinese poem with the following romantic lines: "That we wished to fly in heaven, two birds with the wings of one, and to grow together on the earth, branches of two trees as one." The black and white colors signify the traditional Chinese concept of yin and yang, interpreted in a sculptural, stylized, and minimalist manner.* —SL

Izaskun Zabala

You Are the Pearl of My Universe | 2006

3.6 X 3.4 X 2.3 CM
Steel, brass, freshwater pearl;
bent, soldered

PHOTO BY FRED HATT

THIS SET *conveys a strong feeling of masculine and feminine even though it has a geometric and squared motif.* —TD

Terry Doyle
Wedding Bands | 2006

LARGER, 2.7 X 2.7 X 1 CM; SMALLER, 2 X 2 X 0.9 CM
Gold, silver; charcoal cast, fabricated

PHOTO BY KARL DUKSTEIN

FOR THESE *rings, string was wrapped around textured wax, and then cast in metal.* —KBS

Kit Burke-Smith
String Rings | 1999

LARGEST, 2.5 X 2.5 X 0.5 CM
Sterling silver; cast

PHOTO BY MARK JOHNSTON

Mette Laier Henriksen

*They Clicked and Fit
Perfectly Together* | 2006

2.4 X 2.4 X 0.3 CM
Sterling silver

PHOTOS BY ARTIST

MADE OF *interlocking
pieces that form a flexible
and textured ring.* —YF

Yael Friedman

Marriage As a Puzzle | 2006

0.7 X 2.5 X 2.5 CM
Sterling silver; 3D Rhino
design, cast

PHOTO BY ARTIST

Aram Choi

Puzzle Ring | 2004

2.5 X 5.7 X 3.2 CM
Sterling silver; soldered

PHOTO BY ANYA KIVARKIS

THIS IS *a gold bandage to wear on your wedding ring finger to cover the pale line that remains after a divorce and the removal of a long-worn band: a ring that can both signal and promote healing.* —ADK

Alyssa Dee Krauss
Wedding Band(aid) | 2000

2.2 X 2.2 X 0.8 CM
18-karat gold, garnet

PHOTOS BY ARTIST

Claude Schmitz

Together | 2001

LARGEST, 2 X 2 CM
18-karat gold

PHOTO BY ARTIST

Karin Nir

Yo Yo | 2006

LEFT, 0.7 X 0.5 X 2 CM; RIGHT, 0.9 X 0.4 X 1.4 CM
24-karat gold plated brass, cotton

PHOTO BY ARTIST

Christoph Freier

Undivided Love | 2006

2.2 X 0.8 CM
Sterling silver

PHOTOS BY ARTIST

Cappy Counard
Untitled | 2003

TOGETHER, 2.3 X 2.3 X 1.4 CM
18-karat gold; fabricated

PHOTO BY ARTIST

Geoffrey D. Giles

Trapezoidal Set | 2004

LARGER, 2.4 X 2.4 X 0.7 CM; SMALLER, 2.1 X 2.1 X 0.5 CM

18-karat yellow gold, 18-karat palladium
white gold; married metal, fabricated,
brushed surface embellishments

PHOTO BY TAYLOR DABNEY

Timothy Meier

Mokume Diamond Band | 2006

2.5 X 2.5 X 1.1 CM

Stainless steel, copper, sterling silver;
mokume gane, lathe turned, swedged

PHOTO BY MATTHEW MEIER

Robert Coogan

Mokume Gane Wedding Bands | 2005

EACH, 2.5 X 2.5 X 0.8 CM
22-karat gold, 18-karat gold, silver;
mokume gane, fused

PHOTO BY ARTIST

Wesley Glebe

Untitled | 2006

0.7 X 2 X 0.2 CM
Titanium, 14-karat yellow gold,
rubies, 14-karat white gold

PHOTO BY ARTIST

David A. Casella

Untitled | 2005

2.6 X 1 X 0.3 CM
18-karat yellow gold,
sterling silver, diamonds

PHOTO BY ARTIST

James E. Binnion

Mokume Wedding Ring | 2005

0.7 X 2.2 CM

22-karat yellow gold, iron;
mokume gane, etched

PHOTO BY HAP SAKWA

SYMBOLIC, YET *literal and discrete, one carries the beloved's heart on one's finger.* —SB

Saskia Bostelmann
Circular Hearts | 2006

0.8 X 0.2 X 0.3 CM
18-karat gold; modeled, electrocardiogram
(EKG) reading transfer, wax carved

PHOTO BY ARTIST

Christine Dwane

Band-It | 2006

2.5 X 1 X 2.5 CM
Titanium, 22-karat gold, diamonds;
machined, lathed, inlaid

PHOTO BY BAPTISTE GRISON

Charles Lewton-Brain

Cage Ring | 2005

2.7 X 2.8 X 0.3 CM

Stainless steel, copper, 24-karat gold;
fusion welded, electroformed

PHOTO BY ARTIST

Todd Reed
Untitled | 2006

0.8 X 1.1 CM
18-karat yellow gold, natural colored
brilliant-cut diamonds

PHOTO BY AZADPHOTO.COM

Bettina Huebner
Ring Lifeline 2 | 2006

0.1 X 0.8 X 1.8 CM
18-karat yellow gold; wax filed

PHOTO BY ARTIST

Cynthia Corio-Poli

Mountain Range | 2005

TOP, 2.2 X 0.7 X 0.2 CM; BOTTOM, 1.9 X 0.5 X 0.2 CM

18-karat yellow gold; wax carved, cast

PHOTO BY ARTIST

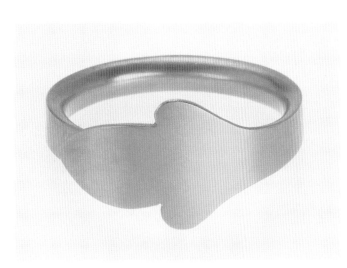

Christa Lühtje

Untitled | 1999

2.2 X 1 CM

22-karat gold; forged, filed, hand fabricated

PHOTO BY EVA JÜNGER

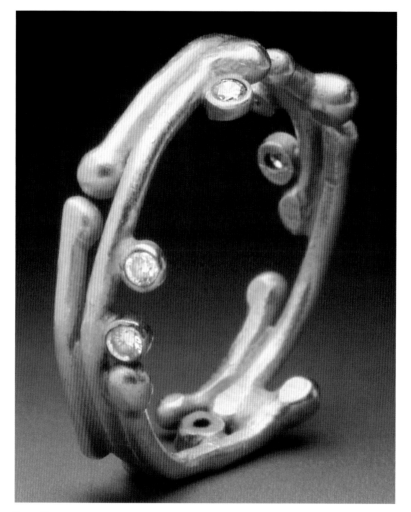

Peg Fetter

Untitled | 2003

2 X 2 X 1 CM

14-karat yellow gold, diamonds;
fused, fabricated, tube set

PHOTO BY DON CASPER

Thomas Herman

Pine Cone Bands and Red Oak Bands | 2005

LEFT, 2 X 2 X 0.8 CM; RIGHT, 2 X 2 X 0.6 CM

18-karat yellow gold; chased, drilled, saw pierced, engraved

PHOTO BY ALLEN BRYAN

Joseph J. Taubenheim

Spiculum Ring #1 | 2006

1.5 X 1 X 1.5 CM

Sterling silver

PHOTO BY ARTIST

Sasha Samuels

Wing Engagement Ring | 2003

2.3 X 2.3 X 1.2 CM

18-karat lemon gold, platinum,
marquise-cut Russian diamond; cast

PHOTO BY DANIEL VAN ROSSEN
COLLECTION OF MRS. WILLIAM STEIN

THIS RING *was designed to flow with the natural contours of the left hand.* —SS

Linda Weiss

Platinum Pavé Band | 2004

2.1 X 2.1 X 1.2 CM

Platinum, 18-karat gold, diamonds;
cast, fabricated, pavé set

PHOTO BY HAP SAKWA

George Sawyer

River | 2006

1 X 2.5 X 2.5 CM

18-karat yellow gold, shakudo,
kuromido; fabricated

PHOTO BY PETER LEE

Ilana Rabinovich-Slonim

My Ring | 2001

2 X 2.5 X 2.5 CM

18-karat gold; hand fabricated

PHOTO BY EREZ AVRAHAM

Chris Ploof

Star Pattern Mokume Ring | 2006

1.9 X 1.9 X 0.5 CM

18-karat yellow gold; diffused bonding
of mokume gane, forged, fabricated

PHOTO BY ROBERT DIAMANTE

Brigid O'Hanrahan

Shibori Rings | 2005

EACH, 1 X 2 X 2 CM

18-karat gold, 22-karat gold;
shibori, soldered

PHOTO BY ARTIST

Garry VannAusdle

Classic Scroll Wedding Bands | 2006

EACH, 1.2 X 1.2 CM

14-karat yellow gold, diamonds;
hard wax carved, lost wax cast,
recarved, stone set

PHOTO BY ARTIST

JACQUELINE IS *a ring made of diamonds from her mother's engagement ring and some additional stones from different life events.* —TK

Tamar Kern

Jacqueline | 2006

2.5 X 2 X 0.6 CM
Diamonds, 18-karat white gold,
18-karat rose gold

PHOTO BY JACQUELINE MARQUE
COURTESY OF ALLOY GALLERY, NEWPORT, RHODE ISLAND

Josephine Bergsøe

In the Sky with Diamonds | 2006

0.3 X 4.5 X 2.5 CM

18-karat gold, 22-karat gold, diamonds;
hand fabricated, soldered

PHOTO BY SARA LINDBAEK

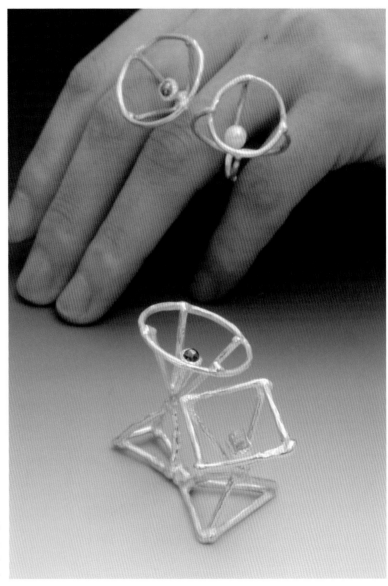

Liaung Chung Yen

Settled Situation | 2005

AVERAGE, 4 X 5 X 3 CM

18-karat gold, brown diamonds, rough
diamond crystal, pearl; fabricated

PHOTO BY ARTIST

THESE RINGS *were designed to work together as a group, just like a couple or a family.* —KDR

Kathleen Diresta-Roth

Stacking Series | 2004

EACH, 5 X 5 CM

Silver, 14-karat gold, 18-karat gold, diamond, peridot

PHOTO BY CHRISTOPHER WEIL

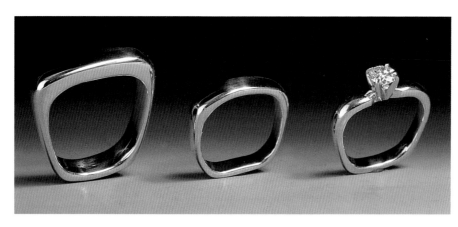

Nancy Slagle

Untitled | 1987

LEFT, 2.1 X 2.1 X 0.5 CM;
CENTER AND RIGHT, 2 X 2 X 0.5 CM

14-karat gold, diamond

PHOTO BY ROBLY A. GLOVER

Michael Zanin

Ring 4x4 (Engagement Ring) | 2005

2.2 X 2.2 X 0.9 CM
18-karat yellow gold

PHOTOS BY ARTIST

Christa Lühtje
Untitled | 2004

2.3 X 1.2 CM
22-karat gold; forged, filed

PHOTO BY EVA JÜNGER

GILDED CAGES *represents my conception of marriage.* —CM

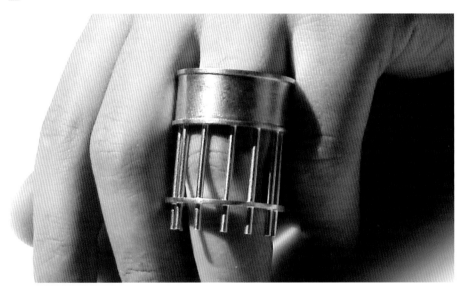

Christophe Marguier
Gilded Cages | 2005

LEFT, 3.5 X 2.6 CM; RIGHT, 3.5 X 2.8 CM
Silver; gilded, constructed

PHOTOS BY ARTIST

TWO PEOPLE *together are more than each single one. Each ring stands on its own and together they form a ball, like the world two people are creating around them.* —CL

Claudia Langer

Spere | 1998

2.4 X 2.4 X 2.4 CM
14-karat yellow gold; cast

PHOTOS BY ARTIST

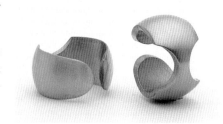

BOTH RINGS *are cut from the same gold sheet. Although they can be separated, they complement each other when united.* —PL

Paula Levy

Happiness | 2006

LARGEST, 1 X 2.2 X 2.2 CM

14-karat gold; hand fabricated, matte finished

PHOTOS BY SANTIAGO CIUFFO

Atsuko Honma

Infinite Track | 2003

2.4 X 4.5 X 0.6 CM

Platinum, white gold, pink gold;
welded, hand carved

PHOTO BY ARTIST

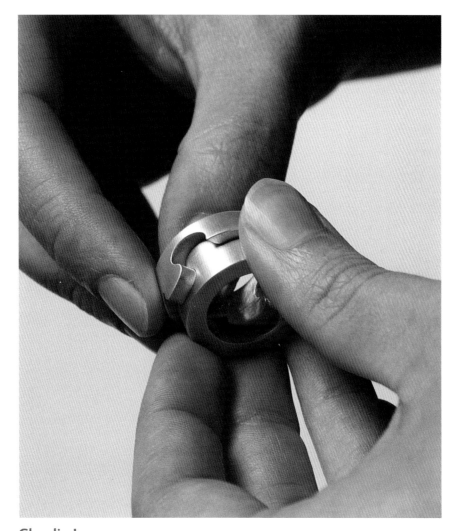

Claudia Langer

Puzzle | 1997

2.4 X 2.4 X 1.2 CM
Silver; cast

PHOTO BY ARTIST

THE UNIQUE *design of this wedding ring invites the addition of a similar ring for every year of marriage. Each additional ring enriches the appearance, while preserving the original character of the design.* —DBD

Dorit Bouskila Dehan
Untitled | 1998

2 X 0.1 X 0.1 CM
22-karat gold; hand fabricated

PHOTOS BY EITHAN SHUKER

Diana Dudek

Untitled | 2004

LEFT, 2 X 2.5 X 1 CM;
RIGHT, 1.8 X 2 X 1 CM

18-karat gold

PHOTO BY ARTIST

Contributing Artists

Aalund, Nanz
Waukesha, Wisconsin
Page 41, 154, 306

Adamson, Marisa
Omaha, Nebraska
Page 73, 99

Alexieva, Tsvetelina
Sofia, Bulgaria
Page 175

Almeida, Maru
Seattle, Washington
Page 76

Ambery-Smith, Vicki
London, England
Page 361

Amendolara, Suzanne
Edinboro, Pennsylvania
Page 357, 363

Arai, Chieko
Cedar Rapids, Iowa
Page 335, 336

Ataumbi, Keri
Sante Fe, New Mexico
Page 153, 231

Avellán, Ami
Degerby, Finland
Page 141, 192

Babikian, Hratch
Philadelphia, Pennsylvania
Page 150, 323

Bally, Boris
Providence, Rhode Island
Page 203, 337

Baran, Colleen
Surrey, Canada
Page 268

Barendse, Pauline
Schoonhoven, Netherlands
Page 193

Barnes, Nick Grant
Silver Spring, Maryland
Page 179

Basharova, Nina
New York, New York
Page 189

Bates, Haley Reneé
Fort Collins, Colorado
Page 255

Behrends, Julia
Boston, Massachusetts
Page 340

Bergsøe, Josephine
Copenhagen, Denmark
Page 304, 315, 404

Bielak, Andrzej
Krakow, Poland
Page 365

Binnion, James E.
Bellingham, Washington
Page 16, 295, 388

Bojczuk, Jessica
Melbourne, Australia
Page 365

Bostelmann, Saskia
Madrid, Spain
Page 389

Bové, Jim
Washington, Pennsylvania
Page 219

Bowden, Jane
Adelaide, Australia
Page 55, 65, 230

Bragsjö, Eva
Solna, Sweden
Page 296

Braham, Frédéric
Antibes, France
Page 200

Brandt, Christine J.
Brooklyn, New York
Page 129, 272

Brevick, Jana
Seattle, Washington
Page 12, 265, 333

Brown, Tavia K.F.
Charlottesville, Virginia
Page 15

Bucci, Doug
Philadelphia, Pennsylvania
Page 338

Burke-Smith, Kit
Cold Spring, New York
Page 266, 375

Bussche, Liesbet
Steendorp, Belgium
Page 330

Carpenter, Tim
Hamtramck, Michigan
Page 69

Carrizzi, Phil
Grand Rapids, Michigan
Page 210

Casella, David A.
San Francisco, California
Page 284, 387

Casuse, Fritz J.
Santa Fe, New Mexico
Page 319

Ceccorulli, Lisa
Hobe Sound, Florida
Page 67

Cheminée, Matthieu
Montreal, Canada
Page 119

Chen, Yu-Chen
Amsterdam, Netherlands
Page 369

Chen, Yuh-Shyuan
Tainan, Taiwan
Page 218, 275

Cheng, Li-Sheng
Dunsden, England
Page 152

Chervitz, Randi
Saint Louis, Missouri
Page 61

Choi, Aram
Eugene, Oregon
Page 377

Choi, Ji Hoon
Seoul, Korea
Page 72

Chung, Jeemin
Seoul, Korea
Page 364

Clausen, Jens
Kautokeino, Norway
Page 48, 201

Coddens, Laura
Bristol, Tennessee
Page 33

Cohen, Barbara
Vancouver, Canada
Page 62

Coogan, Robert
Smithville, Tennessee
Page 385

Cools, Sabrina
Amsterdam, Netherlands
Page 47

Cooperman, Andy
Seattle, Washington
Page 42, 169, 302

Corio-Poli, Cynthia M.
Alexandria, Virginia
Page 237, 393

Counard, Cappy
Edinboro, Pennsylvania
Page 30, 382

Crawford, Matthew J.
Colorado Springs, Colorado
Page 236

Cucchi, Cláudia
Sao Paulo, Brazil
Page 332

Cust, Robin
Siddington, Maine
Front flap, bottom; page 7, 229

Daggett, Jan
Sisters, Oregon
Page 160, 245, 311

Daher, Deborrah
St. Louis, Missouri
Page 10, 176

Darway, C. Christopher
Lambertville, New Jersey
Page 184

Davies, Esther
Berkeley, California
Page 6, 157

Dean, Michael
Vancouver, Canada
Page 152

Deckers, Peter
Upper Hutt, New Zealand
Page 187

Dehan, Dorit Bouskila
Moshav Amikam, Israel
Page 247, 414

Desjardins, Joseé
Canton De Hatley, Canada
Page 309

Dhein, Christine
San Francisco, California
Page 53, 338

Diresta-Roth, Kathleen
Sea Cliff, New York
Page 311, 406

Dogoe Santos, Ana Maria
Bogota, Colombia
Page 225

Doremus, Sarah
Deer Isle, Maine
Page 139

Doyle, Joe Casey
Columbus, Ohio
Page 196

Doyle, Terry
Fort Collins, Colorado
Page 374

Dudek, Diana
Munich, Germany
Page 415

Dwane, Christine
Brossard, Canada
Page 224, 390

Eid, Cynthia
Lexington, Massachusetts
Page 112, 298

Eliseu, Marta Boino
Amsterdam, Netherlands
Page 98

Elyashiv, Noam
Providence, Rhode Island
Page 166

Acknowledgments

We are deeply appreciative of all of the jewelers who submitted images for this publication. Without their willingness to share their talent with Lark Books and its readers, we could never have created this book. We are consistently amazed and inspired by their imagination, innovation, and dedication to the medium.

A warm thank you to the galleries, guilds, and schools that vigorously promote and enrich the field of contemporary jewelry. They contributed immeasurably to disseminating information about this book and to ensuring the volume of submissions we received.

We're indebted to our exceptional assistant editors, Cassie Moore and Mark Bloom, for their careful attention, determination, and good humor. Thanks to Rosemary Kast for being such a friendly and helpful front line. Dawn Dillingham is the true superhero of Lark 500 books, processing thousands of entries, organizing copious amounts of slides and digital images, generating captions, and staying on top of absolutely everything. You all amaze us and work miracles daily.

Thank you to our wonderful art department. To Jackie Kerr for the creative design and layout; to Shannon Yokeley for being willing to work side-by-side and spread-by-spread; to Lance Wille for keeping it all on schedule; to Chris Bryant for developing and maintaining such a splendid visual style; and to Cindy LaBrecht for her lovely jacket design. We couldn't ask for a better team or a better package.

Marthe Le Van